Presidents and Their Pens

The Story of White House Speechwriters

James C. Humes

INTRODUCTION BY JULIE NIXON EISENHOWER

Hamilton Books

An Imprint of
Rowman & Littlefield
Lanham • Boulder • New York • Toronto • Plymouth, UK

Copyright © 2016 by Hamilton Books
4501 Forbes Boulevard, Suite 200, Lanham, Maryland 20706
Hamilton Books Acquisitions Department (301) 459-3366

Unit A, Whitacre Mews, 26-34 Stannary Street,
London SE11 4AB, United Kingdom

Library of Congress Control Number: 2015960141
ISBN: 978-0-7618-6727-2 (pbk : alk. paper)—ISBN: 978-0-7618-6728-9 (electronic)

♾™ The paper used in this publication meets the minimum requirements of American
National Standard for Information Sciences Permanence of Paper for Printed Library
Materials, ANSI/NISO Z39.48-1992.

Contents

Introduction

Julie Nixon Eisenhower

The presidency continues to fascinate Americans, and there are few writers on the scene today who have observed first-hand more presidencies than James Humes. He first assisted Dwight D. Eisenhower and he went on to work with four more presidents. Now, with the publication of his thirty-eighth book, *Presidents and Their Pens*, history enthusiasts have an important new window into how presidents lead and communicate their vision through major speeches.

In the memorable words of Theodore Roosevelt, the presidency is a "bully pulpit." The ability to speak well and persuasively is one of the most powerful tools of leadership and therefore one of the most important skills presidents have to master. But our leaders do not master this skill by themselves. As James Humes vividly illustrates, public speaking is in fact an interactive process not only between speaker and audience, but also between speaker and speechwriter. With the dramatic tension that Humes brought to his four books on Winston Churchill, perhaps the greatest orator of the twentieth century, the author delves into the stories of how presidents work with their assistants to find the precise words to explain or even immortalize a policy or event. From George Washington to Barack Obama, James Humes documents how words have moved our democracy forward.

It has been my privilege to know the creative and indefatigable James Humes for more than half a century. He is a writer whose deep knowledge of and love for speech has shaped every book—and shapes every conversation. *Presidents and Their Pens* is an important addition to the ever-expanding library of literature on the presidency.

Chapter One

George Washington's Farewell Address

The only speech that is required by law to be read every year is one that was actually drafted by a presidential speechwriter. It wasn't so much a speech but an eighteenth-century version of today's op-ed article that was printed in the *American Daily Advertiser* on September 17, 1796. It was passed out in the streets of Philadelphia as President Washington's carriage was rolling home to Mount Vernon.

The idea of a valedictory was first suggested to him by James Madison at the end of his first term. But Washington yielded to his sense of duty and decided to serve for another four years. He felt that the Republic was too fragile to weather his departure, since conflict between France and Britain threatened to embroil the young nation.

Of all the heroic qualities Washington possessed, a thick skin was not one of them. A proud man, he was sensitive to the innuendos and calumnies bruited about by the partisans of Thomas Jefferson's fledgling Democratic-Republican Party. Washington had once admired his fellow Virginian plantation owner. He had valued Jefferson's erudition and he had appointed him his secretary of state when Hamilton was pushing John Jay for the number-one cabinet post. Jay, who had been Hamilton's co-author of the *Federalist Papers*, had served as foreign secretary under the Articles of Confederation.

But Washington had become estranged from his fellow Virginian, who played the anti-Royalist card in his campaign to build up his new party in the young nation. Washington remembered how Jefferson had once implored him to run again in 1792. Jefferson, at that time, had feared that the vice president, John Adams, would succeed the General as Chief Executive. Now Jefferson was telling his political friends that Washington's decision to run again proved his monarchal ambitions.

Jefferson's mouthpiece in his State Department described Washington's receptions and levées at the Executive Mansion as regal in their pomp and court ceremony. This anti-patrician pose of Jefferson's galled Washington, for Jefferson, in his little palace at Monticello, was presiding over multi-course banquets and serving French claret and brandy.

Unlike his minions John Beckley and William Duane, Jefferson did not directly attack the popular president. He did, however, write to his Italian friend, Felipe Mazzei, of Washington's being a Samson shorn by the harlot England.

When Washington set down his thoughts in 1796, he wrote that he had done his best and noted that he had arrived at an age when retirement was necessary and that in any case rotation in office helps sustain liberty. He then came to his central concern: a warning that the country should avoid unnecessary alliances. What followed was a bitter outburst from the usually stoic Washington. He penned a spate of words that only proved what they tended to deny.

> As this address, Fellow citizens, will be the last I shall ever make you, and as some of the Gazettes of the United States have teemed with all the Invective that disappointment, ignorance of facts, and malicious falsehoods could invent, to represent my politics and affections; to wound my reputation and feelings; and to weaken, if not entirely destroy the confidence you have been pleased to repose in me, it might be expected at the parting scene of my public life that I should take some notice of such virulent abuse. But, as heretofore, I shall pass them over in utter silence. . . . [1]

He then added angrily:

> I did not seek the Office with which you have honored me, that charity may throw her mantle over my want of abilities to do better; that the gray hairs of a man who has . . . spent five and forty years, all in the prime of his life, in serving his country, be suffered to pass quietly to the grave; and that his efforts, however numerous, if they are not criminal, may be consigned to the Tomb of oblivion, as he himself soon will be to the Mansions of Retirement.

Washington closed by saying he had not served his country from ambitious views. His finances had received no augmentation from his country.

> I leave you, he wrote, with undefiled hands, an uncorrupted heart and with ardent vows to heaven for the welfare & happiness of that country in which I and my forefathers to the third and fourth Ancestry progenitor drew our first breath. [2]

If this angry and defensive message albeit in the formalistic language of the eighteenth century is not quite the equivalent of Nixon saying, in 1974, I am not a crook, it is reminiscent of the 1962 Nixon press conference after his gubernatorial defeat, when a tired and exhausted Nixon blurted: You won't have Dick Nixon to kick around any more.

Washington had shared Hamilton's vision of a commercial and manufacturing America. He chose Hamilton's view of America's future, not Jefferson's of small farmers. Hamilton had returned from his Treasury Office in Philadelphia to his New York law office. The forty-year-old Hamilton must have winced as he read the letter packet from President Washington. For the disciplined General to give vent to such an emotional tirade was untypical. The essence of Washington was his bearing, the fixed blue eyes that instilled in people a sense of awe. He had a height and stature comparable to that of Charles de Gaulle in the last century. Washington was not unaware of his leadership looks, and he sensed early in his career that any lapse of demeanor would detract from his authority.

So for Washington to leave exposed his anguish and vulnerability in his Farewell Address was disturbing to Hamilton. The defensive outburst may make Washington more human to contemporary eyes, but to Hamilton then, it made him less heroic. The General should not descend from his Olympian heights to the level of mere mortals.

Hamilton was the arch-foe of Jefferson's new Democratic-Republican Party. Hamilton was a Federalist but even more so an imperialist, the first in America. He was the bastard son of a Scottish merchant and his Creole mistress. Hamilton had no roots in the colonies. He was not a Virginian like Washington or a Massachusetts man like John Adams. He was an American.

Plato may have idealized the philosopher-king but Hamilton's ideal would have been the philosopher-general. The figure who came closest to that in the eighteenth century was Frederick the Great. In an age when some rulers valued erudition only second to empire, Frederick could lay claim to being the Age of Enlightenment's most enlightened king. The soldier's writings that lay on Hamilton's shelf in New York City seemed to be an apt guide to the tenor of his own General's farewell remarks. Frederick had written not a valedictory but a testament. It was an attempt to control the course of Prussian foreign policy from the grave.

Washington realized on reading Hamilton's draft that it was right to scrap his emotional defense. Washington also agreed with Hamilton's statement that the central government must be strong enough to withstand the enterprises of faction. Washington left untouched Hamilton's assertion on the importance of establishing public credit. He also left intact the key phrases of Hamilton's principles of foreign policy.

In Washington's request of him to fashion the draft of a Farewell Address, Hamilton saw an opportunity to write a political equivalent of a last will and testament. By making the Farewell Address a set of foreign policy principles, he could finesse Washington's defensive outburst.

The first problem was how to begin—or rather how to turn farewell sentiments into foreign policy principles. As a practicing trial lawyer, Hamilton knew how to establish the authority of a star witness. Here Hamilton was raising Washington above the political controversies of the day and imputing to him the lofty objective that only disinterest in office and denial of any further ambition can impart.

Washington had advised neutrality on the basis of his experience. Hamilton would lift it to the realm of political science. What seemed practical to Washington was treated by Hamilton as immutable principle. In revising Washington's first draft for a valedictory, Hamilton transformed it into a political testament.

> Excessive partiality for one nation and excessive dislike for another cause those whom they actuate to see danger only on one side, and serve to veil and even second the arts of influence on the other. [. . .] The Great rule of conduct for us in regard to foreign Nations is in extending our commercial relations to have with them as little political connection as possible. [3]

Then Washington would put his imprimatur on Hamilton's geo-political insight:

> Europe has a set of primary interests, which to us have none or a very remote relation. Hence she must be engaged in frequent controversies, the causes of which are essentially foreign to our concerns. [. . .] Our detached and distant situation invites and enables us to pursue a different course. If we remain one People, under an efficient government, the period is not far off when we may defy material injury from external annoyance; when we may take such an attitude as will cause the neutrality we may at any time resolve upon to be scrupulously respected—when belligerent nations, under the impossibility of making acquisitions upon us, will not lightly hazard the giving us provocation; when we may choose peace or war, as our interest guided by justice shall counsel. [4]

Washington grasped Hamilton's reasoning that our special geography afforded us a diplomatic advantage.

> Why forego the advantages of so peculiar a situation? Why quit our own to stand upon foreign ground? Why, by intertwining our destiny with that of any part of Europe, entangle our peace and prosperity in the toils of European ambition, rivalship, interest, humour or caprice? [5]

But Washington did not realize from Hamilton's draft that he was positioning himself as the patriarch passing down the tablet for the ages. Rather, he saw himself as an elder statesman guarding his most important accomplishment: the Act of Neutrality of 1793. But actually the words in time became the Gospel of Saint George with Hamilton as the apostle writing the epistle. That is why Congress felt obliged to require future Congresses to be read aloud the scripture.

Jefferson would paraphrase it in his First Inaugural, saying no entangling alliances. Monroe would codify it in the Monroe Doctrine. Later foreign policy statements of both Polk and Cleveland would be rooted in this Farewell Address. Woodrow Wilson would interpret no entangling alliances as no covert alliances. Franklin Roosevelt would take no entangling alliances as no alliances with the Axis as a justification for the Lend Lease Act of 1941.

If Alexander Hamilton is the first presidential speechwriter, he also may be the greatest. He took the authority and prestige of George Washington to engrave a cornerstone of American foreign policy for the ages.

NOTES

1. George Washington, Washington's Farewell Address, quoted in James C. Humes, *My Fellow Americans: Presidential Speeches That Shaped History* (Westport, CT: Praeger, 1992), 4.

2. Ibid.
3. Ibid., 11.
4. Ibid.
5. Ibid.

Chapter Two

Thomas Jefferson — A Revolutionary Becomes a Reconciler

The author of the Declaration of Independence would never ask for writing assistance. It would have been beneath him. But if he ever needed advice or counsel it would have been for the first speech he ever delivered as president. Anything less than a masterful address could have doomed his presidency before it started. The country was poised for a civil war. A quirk in the Constitution had deadlocked the Electoral College. Presidential candidate Thomas Jefferson was tied with his vice-presidential running mate, Aaron Burr. Under the Constitution, in such a close vote, the election had to be determined by the House of Representatives.

Amid rumors of various political plots, such as the Federalists throwing some votes to Burr in the House of Representatives, or their installing Chief Justice John Washington Marshall as an interim president, Jefferson rode on horseback to the new capital in Washington. On that December journey, Jefferson tried to make some sense of the political maelstrom he was riding into. The House of Representatives, who now had the responsibility of se-lecting the next president, were divided between two political parties, the Federalists and the Democratic-Republicans. They were also then subdivided into warring factions among themselves: the "High Federalists," who saw Jefferson as the High Priest of French Revolutionary Jacobinism, and the more moderate Federalists, who might accept Jefferson with the right deal.

Then his own party was split between himself and Burr. The first thing Jefferson did was call on President Adams, who bitterly informed him, "You threw me out." So any advice of Adams to denounce the scheme of installing Marshall was out.

Jefferson was left only with calling on his archenemy for over a decade, Alexander Hamilton, the leader of the Federalists. His only hope was that

Hamilton's hatred of his fellow New Yorker, Burr, might influence him toward Jefferson.

Meanwhile, Maryland's state militia was arming themselves for a possible fight against Virginia to the south. There, Jefferson's Commonwealth had called out their militia to ring the southern border of the new Capital. Sentiments on both sides were raging and boiling. To many, the end of twelve years of Federalists was an uprising against the government. The framers of the Constitution were just about all Federalists, including the late George Washington. Jefferson represented a radical change. Some Federalists even buried their Bibles in their hysterical fear of godless doctrines imported from revolutionary France.

On Inauguration Day, Jefferson dressed plainly in contrast to Washington and walked from his boarding house to the Capitol with a group of friends. There was no procession. The only flourish was a company of artillery that discharged a cannon in salute.

Jefferson was no orator like his fiery Virginia contemporary, Patrick Henry. He was a better writer of words than deliverer of them. Yet the fate of the young Republic might now rest on his Inaugural Address. The volatile militia on both sides of the Potomac only needed a spark to ignite armed conflict that would fracture the fragile republic.

The domeless Capitol above was perhaps a metaphor for the unfinished union. When the outgoing president refused to join him at the platform, it was a signal to the Federalists to keep their powder dry. The incoming vice president, Aaron Burr, did not greet Jefferson. After his cousin Chief Justice Marshall, with whom he did not share pleasantries at the Senate Chamber, administered the oath, Jefferson spoke.

Diehard Federalists in the packed chamber waited with apprehension for the words from this champion of revolutionary France. He surprised them with this arresting statement: "We are all *r*epublicans, we are all *f*ederalists."[1]

The listeners present heard the words with capital letters…Republican and Federalist…even if his text had them in lower case. In a literal sense he was referring not to the names of the two parties, but to two political science terms denoting two different philosophical approaches to government. It was Jefferson's novel insight that the two terms were not mutually exclusive.

He was telling the Americans to reject the institution of monarchy and the imperialistic tyranny of aristocratic rule. At the same time, he agreed that some consideration of government authority was necessary to hold together the fragile confederacy of the fifteen sovereign states. Jefferson then added a sentence that was Miltonic in its simplicity and brilliance:

> If there be any among us who wish to dissolve this Union or change its republican form, let them stand undisturbed, as monuments of the safety with which error of opinion may be tolerated where reason is left free to combat it. [2]

Jefferson's tone was dry and matter-of-fact, but the lucid analysis makes the Inaugural Address stand with the *Federalist Papers* as one of the seminal documents on American government. What Jefferson is saying is that our political heritage is both the Constitutional "Union" and the Bill of Rights.

Jefferson had never been an eloquent master of the spoken word, but for once his dry dispassionate delivery enhanced the impact of his statement. The theme was not that of a rallying cry but that of reconciliation. The audience that strained to hear his measured sentences was more ready to ponder its message.

The more moderate of the Federalists were impressed by the magnanimity of tone. Not a note of chilling lecture or gleeful triumph intruded to sharpen any of his phrases to a partisan edge. Yet in the olive branch extended to the 'moderate' Federalists there was a stick apparent to those who would study the written text in later days. The audience heard "Federalist," but actually he was only saying that all Americans are supporters of the Constitution. In the same way, he pledges to the Federalist opposition an administration that would respect their minority interests.

> Though the will of the majority is in all cases to prevail, that will to be rightful must be reasonable; that the minority possess their equal rights, which equal law must protect, and to violate would be oppression. [3]

Yet a closer scrutiny reveals a subtle if pointed reminder that his presidency would never resort to any legislation like the Adams administration's Alien and Sedition Act.

Jefferson took care to mute the revolutionary rhetoric that filled his earlier letters and campaign talk, but he did not sacrifice to the interests of unity his Republican conception of the elect government.

> A wise and frugal government, which shall restrain men from injuring one another, shall leave them otherwise free to regulate their own pursuits of industry and improvement, and shall not take from the mouth of labor the bread it has earned. This is the sum of good government, and this is necessary to close the circle of our felicities. [4]

What disdain Alexander Hamilton must have felt as he listened to Thomas Jefferson respond to the doctrine of limited government! But the constituents that Jefferson championed—artisans, backwoodsmen, small farmers, and even plantation owners on the scale of Monticello—would have little need for a federal government that was anything more than a disinterested policeman or a remote or unexacting landlord.

If Washington was the first president who saw himself as an American, Thomas Jefferson was the first to see Americanism as democracy. In 1776 Thomas Jefferson wrote more than a rationale for rebellion; he introduced a revolutionary creed: "All men are created equal."

To Jefferson a federal government that consolidated authority at the expense of the state or abridged liberty at the expense of individuals was betraying its special mission in history. And a federal government that saw its role as a promoter of business and commerce in the coastal cities would reduce the influence of those who worked their fields by hand. The "democrats" in Jefferson's day were the farmers and frontiersmen. They made up a class unique to America and, as such, they were to him the real Americans.

To Constitutional purists, it comes as a surprise that the champion of limited powers to the federal government would broaden that authority to negotiate the Louisiana Purchase. But Jefferson's belief in democracy presupposed a democratic way of life. And only in a nation of ample scope would his kind of Americans, the pioneers and future farmers, find room to build their own future and carve their own destiny.

In iambic lines that almost suggest a patriotic hymn, he intoned:

> A rising nation, spread
> Over a wide and fruitful land . . .
> Advancing rapidly to destinies
> Beyond the reach of mortal eye.[5]

In words that Lincoln would later echo, Jefferson then described as "the world's best hope" this freedom offered in the open lands of the New World. If his speech was more style than substance and should be valued more for its immediate impact than its substantive message, it brought stability to a divided nation on the verge of a civil conflict. Jefferson the revolutionary triumphed as a reconciler.

NOTES

1. Humes, *My Fellow Americans*, 23.
2. Ibid.
3. Ibid., 24.
4. Ibid.
5. Ibid., 25.

Chapter Three

James Monroe Defines
U.S. Foreign Policy

If drafting a major address for the chief executive is a criterion, then John Quincy Adams qualifies as a presidential speechwriter. That being the case, Adams is the most erudite and literal individual to ever pen pieces for the president.

John Quincy Adams was a Phi Beta Kappa from Harvard who would write and converse in many languages. The son of the second president came to head the State Department in the administration of James Monroe. He had qualifications for the top diplomatic post exceeded by none at the time or since. The new secretary of state had spent much of his formative life in Europe, initially as the son and secretary of John Adams in his diplomatic assignments. Later he earned his own foreign policy credentials as a minister to the Netherlands, Russia, and Britain.

Adams was aware that previous secretaries of state like Jefferson and Madison had been elected president, but he had rivals in the cabinet ready to contest him for accession to the White House, including Secretary of the Treasury William Crawford and Secretary of War John C. Calhoun. Outside the Executive Branch, Speaker of the House Henry Clay also entertained presidential ambitions.

Watching their maneuvering was James Monroe, one of the so-called Virginia Dynasty of Presidents. Washington, "the Father of his Country," had his Farewell Address, which must be read to Congress every session. Thomas Jefferson was the writer of the Declaration of Independence, and James Madison was deemed the real author of the Constitution. But Monroe was the only president besides the iconic George Washington who actually fought in the Revolution.

In the famous painting of Washington crossing the Delaware, Monroe is pictured at the helm of the boat. He would later be injured at Trenton. In addition, his 6'2" stature and rugged looks resembled those of Washington. Monroe would try to foster that image as president by wearing the wig, white stockings, and breeches of Washington long after they went out of style. If Washington still called himself "General," as president, Monroe liked others to address him as "Colonel Monroe," the rank he achieved in the war.

President Monroe believed himself to be the linear heir of George Washington. Now that his administration was drawing to action, Monroe felt that something more than a speech was needed to continue and enlarge on Washington's Farewell Address and Jefferson's First Inaugural.

John Quincy Adams was aware of Monroe's grandiose ambitions but apprehensive that such a manifesto might draw America into the maelstrom of European politics.

If Monroe wanted to be acclaimed as the advocate of Americanism, he did not want to be held accountable as an architect of war. He remembered how Northerners referred to the War of 1812 as "Mr. Madison's War." Monroe took seriously the characterization of his tenure as "The Golden Age of the Republic."

Caught between the dangers of war and the demands of nationalism, Adams' boss vacillated. How could the President of the United States be both a keeper of peace and a champion of freedom? It was a tug between present risk and future reputation. In the end he chose to sacrifice peace for posterity.

So Monroe decided to issue a non-interference warning to Europeans, but at the same time to support the revolting Greeks against the Turks. Old World controversies should not obstruct the emerging republics of Latin America, but Greece, the cradle of democracy, must also be championed.

They were noble sentiments, thought Adams, but if he placated Monroe and used those as a basis for a pronouncement, the chief executive might pilot the ship of state onto a reef and shoals of power politics among the big European nations.

Adams, like Jefferson, believed that American interference in Europe was just as wrong as European interference in America.

> The ground I wish to take [recommended Adams] is that of earnest remonstrance against the interference of the European powers by force in South America, but to disclaim all interference on our part with Europe; to make an American cause, and adhere inflexibly to that. [1]

In the meantime, the British were forcing the American hand. Their Foreign Secretary George Canning asked our envoy Richard Rush in London to join with the British in a signed statement against any attempt by European powers to restore the rule of Spain in her former colonies. Britain, who had opened up trading markets in those new independent colonies, wanted Spain to keep hands off.

But to join the British in a warning against Europeans went against the grain of Monroe's fiber. After all, Washington's parting testament was not to embroil American foreign policy in European intrigue.

Adams had dealt with Canning before. In a conversation with the Foreign Office diplomat, he accused the British of laying claim to every place under the sun.

"You claim India; you claim Africa."

"Perhaps a piece of the moon," Canning said sarcastically.

"No," said Adams. "I have not heard you claim exclusively any part of the moon, but there is not a spot on this habitable globe that I could affirm you don't claim."[2]

Adams, however, was not hostile to the Canning proposal. Yet he did insist that the Americans go it alone. He lectured his own cabinet.

> It would be more candid to avow our principles explicitly to Russia and France than to come in as a cockboat in the wake of the British man o'war.[3]

Speaker Clay sounded alarmed against some sort of old-time Holy Alliance invasion of America. Adams thought the notion was absurd and Adams' view prevailed in the Cabinet. Rush, in London, was instructed to reject the Canning proposal.

But Adams had to come up with something to satisfy the romantic idealism of the president. Adams then found a way for his president to have his pronouncement, but have it voiced to Congress, not abroad.

In this way, Monroe would have his Doctrine for the history books, but not set off warning bells in Europe.

December 1823 was time for the president's Annual Message to Congress. Adams would slip into paragraphs for roads, post offices, and tariffs key lines of the Monroe Doctrine.

The secretary of state had his work cut out for him. In the fifty-two-paragraph statement, only three paragraphs constituted what is the Monroe Doctrine. Into this ponderous review of the nation's state of affairs, Adams inserted two warnings to Europe. The first "sandwiched-in" provision came in the seventh paragraph—the non-colonization section.

A lengthy paragraph begins by discussing negotiation with the Russians and the British on their respective rights, and interests of the United States and Britain on the northwest coast of North America. The paragraph ends with this clause:

> . . . that the American continents, by the free and independent condition which they have assumed and maintain, are henceforth not to be considered as subjects for future colonization by any European powers. [4]

In the statement up to the forty-ninth paragraph, the message dwelt on such monumental topics as repairs on the Cumberland Road, improvements in the postal service, the protective tariff, and the new U.S. Military Academy. Then Adams sneaked in a mention of the Greek question. The diplomat weakened Monroe's warning to a wish:

> A strong hope has been long entertained, founded on the heroic struggle of the Greeks, that they would succeed in their contest and resume their equal station among the nations of the earth. [5]

With that statement, Adams watered down Monroe's original call for support to an expression of good wishes. American involvement in Europe was carefully proscribed to set up the warning to Europe not to meddle in the Americas.

The rest of the Monroe Doctrine continued in the fiftieth and fifty-first paragraphs. The key sentence in the fiftieth reads:

> We owe it, therefore, to candor and to the amicable relations existing between the United States and those powers to declare that we should consider any attempt on their part to extend their system to any portion of this hemisphere as dangerous to our peace and safety. [6]

In the fifty-first paragraph, Adams lays down the rationale of this non-interference principle:

> Our policy in regard to Europe . . . is, not to interfere in the internal concerns of any of its powers; to consider the government de facto as the legitimate government for us; to cultivate friendly relations with it, and to preserve those relations by a frank, firm, and manly policy, meeting in all instances the just claims of every power, submitting to injuries from none. But in regard to those continents circumstances are eminently and conspicuously different. [7]

Then Adams expounds on the non-interference principle:

> It is impossible that the allied powers should extend their political system to any portion of either continent without endangering our peace and happiness; nor can anyone believe that our southern brethren, if left to themselves, would adopt it of their own accord. It is equally impossible, therefore, that we should behold such interposition in any form with indifference. [8]

The words were Adams' but they reflected the views of Monroe and all Americans. If the British foreign secretary first advanced the idea of non-interference by European powers in the Western Hemisphere, it was his American counterpart who specifically originated and spelled out the non-colonization principle.

Adams may have been the first president to use legal not lyrical language, which comprised this address. Leave it to future wordsmiths to write for their presidents like Ted Sorensen or Peggy Noonan, to craft phrases that soared to poetic heights. Adams would, in his crafting of the address, make his chief executive reach the summit of presidential messages.

No president—not even the venerable Washington, the learned Jefferson, or the saintly Lincoln—has a national sacred dogma attached to his name. By his decision to put the Latin American issue in a presidential message, he raised the flag of American foreign policy before the entire world and implanted that flag firmly in the national conscience.

The Monroe Doctrine owes its ingrained popularity to the mythical belief that the Atlantic and Pacific Oceans separate the New World from the Old. It was this belief—that God had singularly blessed this country—that inspired Washington's Farewell Address. The neutrality of Washington was then exported into the hemispheric solidarity of the Monroe Doctrine. Conservatives and liberals have both cited it to advance their programs.

If James Monroe offered immortality through the Doctrine, John Quincy Adams was truly confirmed as prime minister of the cabinet and frontrunner for the presidency in 1824.

NOTES

1. John Quincy Adams, *Memoirs of John Quincy Adams* (Philadelphia: J.B. Lippincott, 1852), quoted in Humes, *My Fellow Americans,* 34.
2. Ibid., 33.
3. Ibid.
4. Ibid. 35.
5. Ibid.
6. Ibid.
7. Ibid., 35–36.
8. Ibid., 36.

Chapter Four

Andrew Jackson, American Folk Hero

Andrew Jackson was the first president to become the cult idol of the American Masons. Jackson was neither an exalted "Father of his Country" like Washington, nor a philosopher king like Jefferson. But to much of the country he was a folk hero. General Jackson was a real American flesh-and-blood champion who embodied the hopes and aspirations of the rising new nation.

In understanding the political personality of Andrew Jackson, three facts in his background stand out. A Tennessean, Jackson was the first Westerner to be president. His roots were neither from the Virginia gentry nor the New England establishment. Second, he was the last president to be born an English colonial subject and his earliest memories were of that conflict to free the colonies from the British yoke. Third, he served as General in the second conflict against the British—a war that the West fervently supported but the New England East opposed.

As the victor in the Battle of New Orleans, General Jackson won instant fame, but never overcame his bitterness against those New England commercial interests that threatened secession at the Hartford Convention.

To Jackson, the royalists of England and the elitists of the East blended into one. He never forgot how they stole the election from him in 1824. War hero Jackson won a plurality of votes, but not a majority, so it went to the House of Representatives. There, Speaker of the House Clay rounded up the votes for John Quincy Adams, who afterward appointed Clay secretary of state. To Jackson, it had the stench of a deal.

His followers were not the bankers and merchants of the coastal East or the big plantation owners of the South. The Jacksonians were the small farmers, the blacksmiths, the laborers, the mechanics, and the frontiersmen who had been incensed by the Adams–Clay defeat of their champion.

If, at first glance, Jackson seemed like a quainter edition of John Wayne, he came across to the adoring crowds of that time like a combination of Daniel Boone and Johnny Cash. Where country music thrives today are the descendants of the Jackson "groupies" of the early nineteenth century. But the real Jackson doesn't quite match the persona. Though he played up his birth in a log cabin, he became squire of a stately plantation in Nashville. He was smeared by the Eastern elite press as an illiterate barbarian; he actually read law as a young man and was elected as a judge.

Jackson sized up men more by their personalities than by their policies. As long as they shared his prejudices against the educated, the elitists, and the East, he accepted them. A populist strain dominated most of his fans.

His inaugural in 1829 confirmed most of his Whig opponents' fears. Jackson partisans, like a bunch of rioting football fans, stormed the White House, breaking china, smashing crystal glasses, spilling punch, muddying the damask chairs, destroying sofas, and pulling down wall hangings. The revelers who felt their hero had been cheated out of the White House in 1824 now flaunted the triumph of the White House against the East. One New England clergyman preached a sermon from Luke 19:41, "Jesus beheld the scene and wept."

The victorious Jackson did not feel like rejoicing. His wife had died during the campaign and Jackson felt the slurs against her that she was a bigamist contributed to her death.

Intrigue in his cabinet about his secretary of war, John Eaton, hardened his attitude against gossipers. The widower Eaton had remarried the buxom Peggy O'Neill, daughter of a Washington innkeeper. Vice President Calhoun's wife refused to receive the "hussy" at their Dumbarton Oaks mansion. Most of the cabinet followed suit except for Secretary of State Martin Van Buren, who was unmarried.

The cabinet began to fragment. Vice President Calhoun headed the States-Righters. At the Jefferson Day dinner on April 13, 1820, the president looked squarely in Calhoun's eye and toasted "Our Federal Union—it must be preserved." The flustered Calhoun took a moment to recover and then responded, "The Union next to liberty most dear." Calhoun would later resign as vice president to be senator again from South Carolina. In a cabinet reshuffle, Jackson would appoint Van Buren to be his minister to Britain. Jackson had two reasons: first to extricate Van Buren from the intra-cabinet squabbling and also to reinforce his foreign policy credentials as a possible future presidential candidate.

As leader of the Whigs, Henry Clay wanted to squelch any aspirations of Van Buren and led the Senate at first to block the nomination. Jackson warned, "In killing a minister, they may have created a future president."

But when Van Buren was later confirmed, his departure from the cabinet gave rise to a "kitchen cabinet"—a group of informal advisers. One of these was Amos Kendall. Kendall was the first speechwriter to be an alter ego for the president. Like Ted Sorensen for JFK, or Ray Price for Richard Nixon, he was the first presidential adviser in history to work mostly as a speechwriter. If Jackson had a cult of followers, Kendall was the most passionate of his devotees. Yet he was the most unlikely subject to become a Jackson fan. He was a former Easterner and Whig. He had attended Dartmouth, the college of Whig stalwart Daniel Webster, and had once been a tutor to the family of Henry Clay! He had left Dartmouth and moved west to take the tutoring job.

It is often said that converts make the most passionate of zealots. Perhaps he saw no "flaming bush" like Paul, but his campaign speeches certainly lacked no fire. The issue would be renewal of the National Bank charter.

If Ray Price represented Nixon's philosophical side, Pat Buchanan manifested his pugnacious. Amos Kendall was a Buchanan-predecessor. The ring of the campaign bell brought out the killer punch in Kendall.

All the Eastern press labels of Jackson just fueled the anger in Kendall. There were snippets about his boyhood when he spat at a Redcoat officer who wanted the youth to black his boots; that Jackson sassed the English captain only enhanced his legend. It was said Jackson enjoyed the killing of Indians. To frontiersmen who believed that the only good Indian was a dead Indian, this made Jackson popular. The fact that he killed in a duel a fellow Tennessee senator who had called his wife a prostitute made him a folk favorite.

As president he was invited to Harvard for a speech. Adams' cousin, Josiah Quincy, an officer of the institute, was aghast. Traditionally, the speaker would speak in Latin at this venerable university. To everyone's surprise, Jackson gave them the only Latin he knew, "E Pluribus Unum, Sinequa Non."

Back in the country, his Jacksonian fans would slap their knees in laughter or play the fiddle and dance a little jig. "Old Andy sure showed those snobs in Boston!"

The National Bank needed to be re-chartered. This Philadelphia bank was the pride and joy of Clay's Whig Party, who had inherited their enthusiasm for the Federalist predecessors. The Bank was the leading lender that made Clay's American system possible. It helped finance the bridges, turnpikes, and canals—the arteries of new businessmen.

In 1832, Clay maneuvered himself to be the presidential nominee of the National Republican or Whig Party. For his running mate, he chose John Sargent, who had little to recommend him for high office other than that he was from the pivotal Keystone state of Pennsylvania and chief counsel to the Bank.

Nicholas Biddle, the head of the Bank, couldn't be more opposite to Jackson. The bluest of Philadelphia bluebloods seemed at first glance an effete example of Eastern breeding. He wrote poetry as a hobby and edited a literary magazine.

In a real sense, the duel between the two men—Jackson, the plantation farmer from the West, and Biddle, the financial wizard from the East—was a replay of the Jefferson–Hamilton conflict.

Amos Kendall, the kitchen cabinet adviser–wordsmith, saw the parallels. If Jefferson was the first to play the class warfare card, Kendall was itching to play the whole deck.

Clay, on the other hand, thought he held all the cards. He had counted his votes—more than enough to ensure passage of the charter. If "King Andy," as the Whig press caricatured Jackson with crown and robes in their party newspaper organ, dared to veto, he would be manifesting the tyranny of a monarch.

The political picture in 1832 seemed bleak. Even his secretary of the treasury leaned towards Jackson signing the measure. But his newly appointed attorney general, Roger Taney, was adamant. He thought it was unconstitutional. Interestingly, Jackson was not so opposed to the "bank" as to the cabal of bankers, big merchants, and certain lawyers who were for the bank.

Amos Kendall's views more than echoed those of his boss; they magnified them. He detested those Eastern elitists. He wanted to smash them to bits.

If there was no Marquess of Queensberry in journalism, Kendall would flaunt his hatred for another English aristocrat. Kendall was practiced in bare-knuckle journalism, and could poke sharp elbows on the clinches and wallop right next to the belt. He began hammering out the Veto Message:

> The powers and privileges possessed by the existing bank are unauthorized by the Constitution, subversive to the rights of states and dangerous to the liberty of people. [1]

Then in an egregious appeal to nationalist prejudice, the message corrected the lie that American dollars would be lining the pockets of foreigners:

> Is there no danger to our liberty and independence in a bank that in its nature has so little to bind it to our country? [. . .] Should the stock of the bank principally pass into the hands of the subjects of a foreign country, and should we unfortunately become involved in war with that country, what would be our condition? [2]

The message then returned to the legal jargon of Taney who cited the legislative history of the Bank, and inserted his spin that the constitutional word "necessary" means needful. Again, Kendall capped the constitutional argument with political claptrap:

So far from being necessary and proper . . . it is calculated to convert the Bank of the United States into a foreign bank, to impoverish our people in a time of peace, to disseminate a foreign influence throughout every section of the Republic, and in war endanger our independence. [3]

The speech was a cut and paste job, combining statutory description with street demagoguery. At its end, any Constitutional pretext was abandoned to the cant of a campaign flyer.

It is to be regretted that the rich and powerful often bend the acts of government to their selfish purposes. [4]

Kendall was sounding the trumpet of a class war, summoning the poor to overthrow the rich, in language echoing Jefferson's Declaration.

When the laws undertake to . . . grant titles and executive privilege to make the rich richer and the potent more powerful, the humble members of society—the farmers, mechanics and laborers who have neither the time nor the means of securing like favors to themselves, have a right to complain of the injustice of their government. [5]

Kendall distorted Taney's constitutional reasoning into political engineering.

There are no necessary evils in government. Its evils exist only in its abuses. [. . .] Many of our rich men have not been content with equal protection and equal benefits, but have besought us to make them richer by act of Congress. [6]

The sentences were Kendall's salvoes launching a class war.

If we cannot at once . . . make our government what it ought to be, we can at least take a stand against all new grants of monopolies and exclusive privileges . . . of the few at the expense of the many. [7]

Amos Kendall had ended Jackson's Veto Message with a cannon shot broadside at Clay and the Whigs.

The Senate under Clay rallied, but could not muster a two-thirds majority to override the veto. The fight then moved from Congress to the country. The newspaper that opposed the veto and favored the Bank caricatured the president as "King Andy" in ermine robes. The partisans of Jackson pictured Nicholas Biddle as "Old Nick" complete with horns and tail.

The Jackson Veto Message was a declaration of class war. It was also a catalyst in recasting the Party of Jefferson that had been gradually co-opted by the establishment during the administration of James Monroe and John Quincy Adams.

The Veto Message did not discuss the need for a national bank. It did not discuss the arguments of soft money against hard. The message was not a financial accounting, but a political counting of where the votes were.

It was no monetary wizard who wrote the bank message but a masterful wordsmith and propagandist. Amos Kendall was the first adviser in the Executive Mansion to be chosen for his skills in writing and public relations. He was the first alter ego who would mirror his boss's hates as well as hopes.

Kendall saw Jackson as the champion of the underdog against the establishment and that his victory gave them hope. He was proud to help his hero in fighting for the little people against the big interests, and by his triumph, he lifted their aspirations. If in one sense the Veto Message was the cant of rank demagoguery, it was also the creed of raw democracy.

NOTES

1. Humes, *My Fellow Americans*, 46.
2. Ibid., 47.
3. Ibid.
4. Ibid.
5. Ibid.
6. Ibid., 48.
7. Ibid.

Chapter Five

Abraham Lincoln's Gettysburg Address

James Baker once remarked that the greatest speechwriter in the White House was his boss, Ronald Reagan. But the "Great Communicator" corrected him: "No, it was Abraham Lincoln."

The proof of truth is the fact that Lincoln wrote the greatest oration in history and yet he was less schooled than any writer who ever penned speeches for the president.

But President Lincoln almost missed his opportunity to deliver this timeless oration: the Gettysburg Address.

It all started right after the July battle when the burial of bodies was too daunting an ordeal for the Gettysburg citizenry. They turned to the federal government, and Union soldiers completed the task. To clean and ship the dead soldiers back to their home states would lengthen the ordeal. The solution was to make Gettysburg the site of a national cemetery.

In that more religious era, the dedication of a cemetery was a sacred rite in the community. The town fathers called upon the greatest speaker of the time. That was not Lincoln, but Edward Everett. The Harvard professor of rhetoric and author of books on it had spoken at countless anniversaries, funerals, memorials, banquets, and cornerstone-layings, but this occasion was to him the culmination of his career. To the invitation issued in August, the populist orator replied that November 29 was his first open date. The Gettysburg committee was disappointed at the November date, but the name of Everett would draw a tremendous crowd to the small town.

Only at the beginning of November was a thought given to the invitation of dignitaries. The name of the president was mentioned and dismissed. The folksy Lincoln might not impart the right note to this sacred event. But then someone offered that the president had never left Washington in this war.

Lincoln, to their surprise, accepted. Immediately, Governor Andrew Curtin was dispatched to the White House to emphasize to the president the religious overtones of this dedication. "Keep it short," was his parting advice to the president. Lincoln nodded.

A speech on the morning of the dedication was a talk Lincoln wanted to give. At the celebration of the victory in Pennsylvania, there was a torchlight parade. Lincoln welcomed the well-wishers, but declined to say anything more than a few words:

> How long ago is it—eighty odd years—since on the Fourth of July for the first time in the history of the world a nation by its representatives assembled and declared as a self-evident truth that "all men are created equal." [. . .] Gentlemen, this is a glorious theme, and the occasion for a speech, but I'm not prepared to make one worthy of the occasion. [1]

In November, Lincoln had barely more than two weeks to prepare his brief remarks before those of the distinguished orator Everett. If Lincoln only had a few years of formal schooling, he was per the Greek word an "autodidact." In other words, he had educated himself. He borrowed books like Grimilaw's *History of the United States.* He also read Shakespeare and Sir Walter Scott.

At his desk in the forest-green wallpapered office lay four books: *The Constitution, The Federal Statutes, Shakespeare, Trevelyan,* and the King James Version of the Bible.

Lincoln was a seasoned trial lawyer and state legislator with a vast experience of stump speaking. But the folksy talk he developed to persuade juries or a stump audience would be the wrong language for such an august occasion. Lincoln decided to use phrasing from the King James Version of the Bible. If the Elizabethan English was majestic, it would also be familiar to his listeners. They attended church every week and read the scripture every night.

Contrary to legend, Lincoln did not scribble the Gettysburg Address on the back of an envelope while on the train to the dedication. It was a methodically prepared address in pencil on white-lined commercial paper. When a sentence appeared in his mind, he would utter it aloud and then commit it to paper. Then he chewed on his pencil stub as he contemplated the next line.

Lincoln had decided early on not to mention names or recount any battlefield action in his short remarks. Instead he wanted to express what the battle was fought for. The president had not polished his words for final delivery. An hysterical Mrs. Lincoln had pleaded with her husband not to leave the bedside of their ailing youngest son, Tad.

During the 65-mile train ride from Baltimore to Gettysburg, Lincoln did pen a succession of key phrases as he tried to memorize and rehearse his delivery. It was this mnemonic device for preparing his delivery that probably gave rise to the myth that he composed the talk on the train. Veterans of the platform circuit often note key phrases on the back of an evening program even though they have earlier written out the whole try.

Lincoln at the Gettysburg podium cast a somber look. Deeply etched lines darkened his face. His voice was resonant but clear. In a strident, flat Midwestern accent, Lincoln began:

Four score and seven years ago . . .[2]

Lincoln opened with the adapted biblical line from Numbers that describes man's longevity. The increase to eighty-seven years stressed to his audience that democracy was a fragile flower that had already outlived the human span. Then Lincoln repeated the sentence he had used when speaking before the Young Men's Lyceum of Springfield, Illinois, in 1838. It must be remembered that Lincoln knew much of the King James Version by heart, particularly the Psalms, Proverbs, the Song of Solomon, and Isaiah, as well as the New Testament Gospels.

. . . our fathers brought forth on this continent, a new nation, conceived in liberty. . . .[3]

With echoes of nativity from both the Old and New Testaments ("conceived in bondage"), Lincoln employed the words "brought forth" and "conceived." A pause before the word "liberty" accentuated it. In the Gospel of Matthew, Mary "brought forth" a child.

Lincoln was the first president to use the word "nation." Before Lincoln, it was "the Union." He would repeat "nation" in his axiom.

Lincoln's allusion to Abraham in the biblical line was deliberate. Lincoln's nickname among the Union soldiers was Father Abraham, and their favorite hymn ended, "We are coming, Father Abraham."

The night before the address, they had serenaded Lincoln outside the home of David Wills, where he was staying. Only when they ceased did Lincoln learn that Tad's fever had broken. Perhaps Lincoln saw in the term "Father Abraham" his own destiny as a father of a nation reborn and dedicated to the proposition that "all men are created equal."

It is noteworthy that to Jefferson, "all men are created equal" was a self-evident axiom; but to Lincoln it was a proposition yet to be proved.

Secretary of State William Seward, the only person to whom Lincoln showed the draft, objected to the word "proposition" as inelegant.

Lincoln, however, from his early learning of Euclid's geometry, often used the word to advance a logical argument.

> Now we are engaged in a great civil war, testing whether that nation, or any
> nation so conceived and so dedicated, can long endure. [4]

Lincoln was comparing the Revolutionary War to establish independence
with the ongoing Civil War to preserve the Union. Lincoln was in effect
asking whether this experiment called democracy could long endure.

> We are met on a great battlefield of that war. We have come to dedicate a
> portion of that field, as a final resting place for those who here gave their lives
> that this nation might live. [5]

Lincoln, the lawyer, who could write extracts and wills, could also be
lyrical with the poetic devices of assonance internal rhyme.

"Gave" and "live" expressed the purpose of the occasion: the dedication
of the National Cemetery. The next use of subtle rhyme explained his avowal
of the futility of doing anything in the way of a commemoration service that
would approach the significance of those fallen soldiers' sacrifice.

> But, in a larger sense, we cannot dedicate—we cannot consecrate—we cannot
> hallow—this ground. The brave men, living and dead, who struggled here,
> have consecrated it, far above our poor power to add and detract. [6]

The next statement is ironic today, but evidently Lincoln felt that it was
not what was said here but what was done here that deserved attention.

> The world will little note, nor long remember, what we say here, but it can
> never forget what they did here. [7]

The phrasing is more poetry than prose. Lincoln then issued a summons to
his audience.

> It is for us the living, rather, to be dedicated here to the unfinished work which
> they who fought here have thus far so nobly advanced. It is rather for us to be
> here dedicated to the great task remaining before us . . . [8]

In his entire political career, Lincoln was dominated by two objectives:
first, to prohibit the extension of slavery, and second, to preserve the Union.

> . . . that from these honored dead we take increased devotion to that cause for
> which they gave the last full measure of devotion— [9]

The repetition of "devotion" was a rhetorical device, but "measure" was a
biblical word prominent in Shakespeare, used to express the ultimate sacrifice by the Union dead.

... that we here highly resolve that these dead shall not have died in vain—[10]

The declaration adds graceful alliteration to the geometric logic that the proposition of democracy must be proved. The last phrase would have been taken from a picture in one of the first books Lincoln ever read, Parson Weems' biography of Washington. At Valley Forge, the graves of the dead— those fallen soldiers—are shown honored with a monument under which appear the words, "That these dead shall not have died in vain."

Those words were ever etched in the ten-year-old Lincoln and he would restate them at Gettysburg Cemetery. While Everett was speaking, Lincoln had penned, in a last-minute addition to the text, "under God."

... that this nation, under God, shall have a new birth of freedom—[11]

Though not a religious man in a formal sense, Lincoln was deeply devout. After his breakfast and before going to his office, Lincoln used to spend twenty minutes in the family library reading a passage from the scriptures, particularly from the Old Testament. Like Washington, Lincoln believed that God had ordained a special role for him.

Before the election, Lincoln had told a supporter, "I know there is a God, and that He hates injustice and slavery. I see the storm coming, and I know that His hand is in it. If He has a place and work for me . . . I believe I am ready."[12] Yet his humility did not allow his belief in God to take on a messianic conviction. When during the war a delegation of clergy called on him and said of the Union cause, "God is on our side," Lincoln answered, "No, the question should always be, 'Are we on His side?'"

The biblical nativity analogy that began with "brought forth" and "conceived in liberty" is now completed. Lincoln, though a profoundly humble man, saw himself projected by destiny to be the father of his country, like Washington. As Washington brought forth the nation from foreign bondage to freedom, Lincoln would bring it from domestic bondage into a more complete freedom.

... and that government of the people, by the people, for the people . . . [13]

This poetic trochée to describe democracy had its origin in a note Lincoln's law partner, William Herndon, had forwarded to the abolitionist Theodore Parker. Herndon had heard Parker deliver a speech at Faneuil Hall in 1851 that contained the words "government over all the people for all the people and by all the people." Lincoln adapted and improved it; Lincoln did not stress the preposition in the manner of later schoolboy recital. The repetition of "people" with these different prepositions has more to do with poetry than polity.

. . . shall not perish from the earth. [14]

"Perish" is both a poetic and a biblical verb. His listeners probably never heard it in everyday conversation. It recalls Proverbs 29:18, a favorite verse of Lincoln's: "Where there is no vision, the people perish."

In Lincoln's belief, unless America kept to its Declaration credo, our democracy would die.

The two-minute address of generally familiar biblical phrases was over before its audience could focus their attention. There was no applause; the crowd was either stunned by the unexpected brevity or perhaps, by the prayer-like poetry.

Lincoln thought he had failed. Seward, his friend in government, agreed.

Yet there were discerning listeners. Everett, the master of rhetoric, said, "I would be glad if I came as near to the central idea of the occasion in two hours as you did in two minutes." [15] His aide, John Hay, who, as a Brown student, planned to be a poet, said, "The President, in a fine, free way, with more grace than is his wont, said his half dozen words of consecration. . . ." [16]

Poet Henry Wadsworth Longfellow praised it as "admirable." [17] Emily Dickinson's friend, editor Samuel Bowles, called it "a perfect gem." [18] George William Curtis, who would become the famous editor of *Harper's Weekly*, said, "The few words of the President were from the heart to the heart. They cannot be read without kindling emotion." [19]

Actually, its brevity rendered the address not only more beautiful, but more unusual. Because the address was only about 270 words, it was possible to reprint it not just in this country, but also in Britain due to its brevity. In an era when the daily newspaper was emerging as a phenomenon, the short address was printed and circulated to millions. Its very size would later encourage generations of schoolchildren to commit it to memory.

Yet not even the most prescient of literary men could foresee that in a hundred years the Gettysburg Address would be included in every anthology of English literature as America's sublime contribution to the world. They could not have anticipated that Winston Churchill would deem it the greatest speech ever delivered.

But it would take a bullet in a theater, a surrender at Appomattox, and the freeing of slaves in countless households to enshrine the name of Lincoln and make his words eternal.

The first time this writer ever heard the Gettysburg Address, he was not yet five. It was read to me by Carl Sandburg in our home in Williamsport, Pennsylvania. Sandburg had been invited to speak at the Women's Club by my mother. He had just finished his massive biography of Lincoln. I was kept at home from kindergarten to hear Lincoln stories by the venerable author.

At one time, I said, "Mr. Sandburg, my mother says you are a famous poet."

"No, Jamie," he replied, "Abraham Lincoln is the great poet because he wrote the great American poem."

NOTES

1. Humes, *My Fellow Americans*, 64.
2. Ibid., 75.
3. Ibid.
4. Ibid.
5. Ibid., 76.
6. Ibid.
7. Ibid.
8. Ibid.
9. Ibid., 77.
10. Ibid.
11. Ibid.
12. Henry Ketcham, *The Life of Abraham Lincoln* (New York: A.L. Burt, 1901), 184.
13. Humes, *My Fellow Americans*, 78.
14. Ibid.
15. Ibid.
16. Ibid.
17. Ibid., p. 79.
18. Ibid.
19. Ibid.

Chapter Six

Grover Cleveland—A Light on a Dark Street

Grover Cleveland would no more delegate the onerous task of drafting a Presidential Message than he would hand over to a deputy the macabre chore of hanging two murderers when he was sheriff of Erie County, New York. Punctilious and honest, he would not let anyone else draft words to be delivered under his name.

In the virtue of integrity, Cleveland was not exceeded by any previous president. Yet this probity did not make him popular. He had not looks to excite, the charm to persuade, or the fame to impress the people. The mustached two-hundred-pound heavyweight was caricatured as a bloated walrus on a cold rock. It was an image in no way charismatic but instead corpulent, not dashing but dour.

Yet this plodding politician would dominate the post-war era like an Andrew Jackson or Franklin Roosevelt. For he presented to an age of rising wealth, developing industry, and expanding markets the one commodity that seemed scarce: honesty. His was an integrity so inviolable that it shone like a beacon in a political world where the corruption of big city machines and big business monopolies darkened the halls of democracy.

It was this rare honesty that propelled Cleveland in three short years from City Hall to the White House. The former sheriff who had gained political prominence by personally hanging two killers had become president.

In one of the most famous nomination speeches in convention history, General Edward Bragg's diatribe against the inclusion of delegates from Tammany Hall, he made an asset of his candidate's lack of likability. "They love him, gentlemen, and they respect him, not only for himself, for his character, for his integrity and judgment and iron will, but they love him most of all for the enemies he has made."[1]

In 1884, the Republicans found the purity of Cleveland's life unassailable, but concentrated on his private. Republicans dug up a bastard child. They hoped Cleveland would deny the charge. In truth, even though both Cleveland and his married law partner had consorted with the mother, an attractive widow in Buffalo, the ever-honest Cleveland, to protect his law partner's family, assumed paternity and agreed to pay for the child's support.

The election was a stalemate between Republican James Blaine, whose public life was stained by Credit Mobilier, and Democrat Cleveland, with his personal-life scandal. The Protestant leaders in New York raised the election cry against Democrats: "Rum, Romanism, and Rebellion." It backfired and Cleveland was elected.

The reform-minded Cleveland alienated Republicans by confronting the biggest, most powerful lobby, the Grand Army of the Republic. For years, Republicans had fattened its pension rolls. It was estimated that one fourth of the new claims were fraudulent.

Cleveland's answer was direct. The pension list should be a roll of honor. The blunt honesty that was his virtue as a statesman was also his fault as a politician. The same was true when he proposed to revise the tariff rates.

This was a day before the income tax, when tariffs were a main source of revenue for the government. To cut the tariffs was in effect to cut taxes for the consumer. It was the American family who bore the burden when they paid higher prices for goods protected by the high tariffs. Cleveland decided to reduce the tariff in the beginning of an election year. The controversial move was courageous.

But even Cleveland's friends thought it was ill-advised. In 1888 it would serve to elect the Republicans, who would impose an even higher protective tariff.

To one fearful adviser, Cleveland lectured:

> Do you remember that I opposed a second term on the ground that human nature being what it is the President would work for his own re-election instead of the country. [2]

And to another, he shrugged:

> What's the use of being elected or re-elected unless you stand for something. [3]

That is not the statement of a politician, but of a statesman.

Cleveland worked on his tariff message to Congress for the better part of three days, writing out his recommendations in pen on legal-size paper.

Although he let his lawyers look at it, the final form was basically his and it was a blockbuster, filling eighteen pages of octavo size. It was the first Presidential Message to Congress devoted entirely to one subject.

Cleveland got to the heart of the matter:

> But our present tariff laws, the vicious, inequitable, and illogical source of unnecessary taxation, ought to be at once revised and amended.[4]

He then assured Congress that he did not intend to let American manufacturers die from exposure to European competition.

> It may be called protection or by any other name, but relief from the hardships and dangers of our present tariff laws should be devised with especial precaution against imperiling the existence of our manufacturing interests.[5]

To those who countered that American workers would be thrown out of their jobs, he added:

> To these an appeal is made to save their employment and maintain their wages by resisting a change. . . . But the reduction of taxation demanded should be so measured as not to necessitate or justify either the loss of employment by the workingman or the lessening of his wages. . . .
>
> But it is notorious that this competition (among America's "domestic producers") is too often strangled by combinations quite prevalent at this time, and frequently called trusts, which have for their object the regulation of supply and price of commodities made and sold by members of the combination. The people can hardly hope for any consideration in the operation of these special schemes.[6]

Cleveland argued his case in a much-quoted line that attacked the doctrinaire protectionists who subscribed to the high tariff as an article of faith, as well as to the idealistic free traders whose gospel was spreading from Britain.

> Our progress toward a wise conclusion will not be improved by dwelling upon the theories of protection of free trade. This savors too much of bandying epithets. It is a condition which confronts us, not a theory.[7]

In concluding his remarks, Cleveland declared:

> I am so much impressed with the paramount importance of the subject to which this communication has thus far been devoted that I shall forego the addition of any other topic. . . .[8]

His focusing of the Presidential Message on a single problem is not the only reason that Cleveland's address is one of the most important documents in history. Cleveland also deserves his status as a great president for realizing that a high tariff was not only a tax on necessities for the American family, but also a tool business cartels could use to gouge the consumer by squeezing the competition.

Cleveland then advanced this central argument—that a high tariff was in effect a tax on necessities.

> Nor can the worker in manufactures fail to understand that while a high tariff is claimed to be necessary to allow the payment of remunerative wages, it certainly results in a very large increase in the price of nearly all sorts of manufactures, which, in almost countless forms, he needs for the use of himself and family.[9]

Cleveland, in a radical motion, denounced the high tariff as the tool of trusts and monopolistic cartels. He had targeted the Jay Goulds and other moguls of big business and had taken the protective tariff from the citadel of sacred dogma into the more open field of national debt. Cleveland's bill would pass the House but not the Senate, whose members, at that time, were elected by the big-business-dominated state senates.

In the 1888 election, Republicans ran General Benjamin Harrison, the grandson of a former president. Harrison, an apostle of protection, lost the popular vote even though he carried the electoral majority. In 1892, Cleveland returned to the White House in a surge of disgust against the monstrously high tariff written by Congressman William McKinley. Cleveland tempered that tariff, but his second term was marked by his stubborn defense of the gold standard against strident demands of the silver-Democrats.

Addressing the Tariff Reform League, the poet and diplomat James Russell Lowell said: "I feel myself strongly attached to Mr. Cleveland as the best representative of the higher type of Americanism that we have seen since Lincoln was snatched from us."[10]

In the tariff message as in all his actions, Cleveland wrote what he believed. He never yielded an inch in the cause of truth and never surrendered an iota of principle to expediency.

Action speaks louder than words. If not eloquent, he had an honesty that glowed like a light on a dark street.

NOTES

1. Paul F. Boller, *Presidential Anecdotes* (New York: Oxford University Press, 1996), 177.
2. Humes, *My Fellow Americans*, 87.
3. Ibid., 90.
4. Ibid.
5. Ibid.
6. Ibid.
7. Ibid., 91.
8. Ibid.
9. Ibid., 90–91.
10. James Russell Lowell, *The Complete Writings of James Russell Lowell: Literary and Political Addresses* (Cambridge, MA: The Riverside Press, 1904), 223.

Chapter Seven

Theodore Roosevelt's
"Big Stick" Speech

Theodore Roosevelt was possibly the most erudite president ever to have occupied the White House, as well as the one with the biggest ego. He had many more books published before he became president than all the other Chief Executives wrote after they left office. He was a Harvard Phi Beta Kappa with a photographic memory who had read thousands of books. One time at a White House dinner he quoted lines to the German Ambassador on his one side from Goethe, and then turned to the French envoy Jean-Jules Jusserand and rattled off words from Rousseau.

Before he came to the White House, he had exchanged correspondence with poets, philosophers, and historians. So it was unimaginable for him to ever employ any aide to write speeches for him. He believed he was brighter and better read than anyone in Washington or academia.

Theodore Roosevelt was the new twentieth century personified. It was like Technicolor replacing the nineteenth century's black and white. There have been presidents more heroic, more handsome, more sainted, and more eloquent than Theodore Roosevelt, but none as charismatic. He had been a soldier, deputy sheriff in the territories, police commissioner in New York, author, explorer, and statesman. But as a politician he was no orator like Daniel Webster and Henry Clay who preceded him, William Jennings Bryan, who was a contemporary, or President Ronald Reagan of the recent yester-year.

"Teddy" Roosevelt was a great speaker. Anyone who liked to speak and had delivered thousands of speeches had to be a practiced performer at the podium. He was at center stage and that's where he liked to be. His daughter, Alice Roosevelt Longworth, repeated to me in 1970 the quip: "At a wedding he wanted to be the bride, at a funeral, the corpse."

Roosevelt, if not sometimes a showoff, was always a showman. It is true irony that he was the only president not to use the first person in an inaugural address, because he courted the camera and lit up for a crowd. If he sometimes thundered like an evangelical preacher, he was no spellbinder. He lacked the emphasis, pause, the right timing, and variance of tone of the master rhetorician. Neither did the always-restless Roosevelt have the patience to craft, phrase by phrase, the lines of a professional wordsmith like Ted Sorensen or Ray Price. Roosevelt had a deaf ear for the poetic devices of alliteration, repetition, and internal rhyme.

Roosevelt's strident staccato voice rattled like a machine gun in a talk. He didn't so much persuade them but bowled them over like pins in an alley. Bluntness was always Roosevelt's hallmark and at the podium his technique was plain, simple, and direct. He had a straightforward formula for getting his message across: Tell them what you are going to say, say it, and then tell them what you have said. Roosevelt was no orator of the William Jennings Bryan school; to Roosevelt, the flourishes of such an oratorical style undermined speaking sincerity and credibility.

In Chicago, on April 2, 1903, the president released his big foreign policy message to the world. It was at a banquet for business leaders to showpiece his extension of the Monroe Doctrine.

In December of the previous year, British and Germans acting in concert had captured four Venezuelan gunboats and blockaded that nation's harbors. Roosevelt had his secretary of state deliver a stern note.

Later, Roosevelt wrote that he feared Germany intended to establish a naval base in Latin America. It was not just Germany, but the possibility of any European country taking control of a Latin American nation that worried Roosevelt.

For this address, Roosevelt gathered all his files and correspondence on the Venezuelan crisis, together with a copy of the Monroe Doctrine. He dictated his speech to his stenographer in the New West Wing of the White House.

At the white-tie hotel dinner in the auditorium (which is still standing and owned by Roosevelt University), he rose after his introduction by Franklin McVeagh, chairman of the formalities, whom six thousand Roosevelt partisans rose to applaud. In his distinctive falsetto voice he chopped out in a matter-of-fact tone the purpose of his address.

> Mr. Chairman, Ladies and Gentlemen: Today I wish to speak to you, not merely about the Monroe Doctrine, but about our entire position in the Western Hemisphere. . . .[1]

His rapid rat-a-tat delivery, which stressed consonants over vowels, became even more pronounced as Roosevelt quickly bore into the heart of the message.

> Ever since the time when we definitely extended our boundaries westward to the Pacific and outward to the Gulf . . . our nation has insisted that because of its primacy in strength among the nations of the Western Hemisphere it has certain duties and responsibilities which oblige it to take a leading part thereon.[2]

And then his voice rose in pitch:

> We hold that our interests in this hemisphere are greater than those of any other European power possibly can be, and that our duty to ourselves and to the weaker republics who are our neighbors requires us to see that none of the great military powers from across the seas shall encroach upon the territory of the American republics or acquire control thereover.[3]

The audience enthusiastically roared their approval to Roosevelt's broadening of the Monroe Doctrine. With the operative words "encroach" and "control," Roosevelt widened the application of the Monroe Doctrine. No more did "interference" or "settlement" define the nature of intolerable European involvement. Any military action in the Western Hemisphere that would lead to a takeover or effective dominance of a nation's government would justify the United States' invoking the Doctrine.

> This policy, therefore, not only forbids us to acquiesce in such territorial acquisition, but also causes us to object to the acquirement of a control which would in its effect be equal to territorial aggrandizement.[4]

Roosevelt paused to let the audience endorse his statement with their hands, and then moved on to the proposed Panama Canal project. By implication he seemed to be suggesting to his audience the dangers to our interests if a European country installed a naval base within sailing reach.

> This is why the United States has steadily believed that the construction of the great Isthmian canal, the building of which is to stand as the greatest material feat of the twentieth century—greater than any similar feat in any preceding century—should be done by no foreign nation but by ourselves.[5]

With his photographic memory, Roosevelt hardly had to look at his text as he expounded. But he did look down a bit as he detailed the terms of the treaty Secretary of State John Hay had signed with Lord Julian Pauncefote of Great Britain in November 1901. Britain had awarded control of the canal project to the United States along with the "exclusive right to regulate and manage it, becoming the sole guarantor of its neutrality."[6]

Roosevelt then proceeded to outline the treaty worked out with the nation of Columbia for completing the construction that had been initiated by a French company. In pardonable but hyperbolic self-praise, Roosevelt boasted:

> These treaties are among the most important that we have ever negotiated in their effects upon the future welfare of this country, and mark a memorable triumph of American diplomacy—one of those fortunate triumphs, moreover, which redound to the benefit of the entire world. [7]

Next, Roosevelt recounted the diplomatic history leading up to the recent crisis in Venezuela. He even read in minute detail to the dinner audience the correspondence between his Secretary of State and the German Ambassador. The purpose was to set the stage for reading again and stressing the Presidential Message of December 3, 1901, which was conveyed to the German government.

> The Monroe Doctrine is a declaration that there must be no territorial aggrandizement by any non-American power at the expense of any American power on American soil. It is in no wise intended as hostile to any nation in the Old World. [8]

Roosevelt once advised his one-time friend, William Howard Taft, on delivering a talk:

> A speech should be a series of posters on the same subject in order to get the idea across and make it stick. . . . You have to iterate and re-iterate until you are pretty well sick of your own voice. [9]

Roosevelt then heeded his own advice. He explained again to his audience the effect of his re-interpretation of the Monroe Doctrine.

> The concern of our government was of course . . . to keep an attitude of watchful vigilance and see that there was no infringement of the Monroe Doctrine—no acquirement of territorial rights by a European power at the expense of a weak sister republic—whether this acquisition might take the shape of an outright and avowed seizure of territory or of the exercise of control which would in effect be equivalent to such seizure. [10]

With his eyes sparkling behind his pince-nez spectacles, his moustache bristling and his teeth flashing as he inhaled, Roosevelt propounded his credo:

I believe in the Monroe Doctrine with all my heart and soul . . . but I would infinitely prefer to see us abandon it than to see us put it forward and bluster about it, and yet fail to build up the efficient fighting strength which in the last resort can alone make it respected by any strong foreign power whose interest it may ever happen to be to violate it. [11]

Roosevelt continued pounding his sermon from "the bully pulpit."

Boasting and blustering are as objectionable among nations as among individuals, and the public men of a great nation owe it to their sense of national respect to speak courteously. [. . .] But though to boast is bad, and causelessly to insult another, worse, yet worse than all is it to be guilty of boasting, even without insult, and when called to the proof to be unable to make such boasting good. [12]

Here Roosevelt pulled out his brightest poster.

There is a homely old adage which runs: "Speak softly and carry a big stick; you will go far." [13]

Roosevelt had first used the motto to explain in a conversation how he handled Tom Platt's Republican machine. Shortly before he became president, he introduced it at the Minnesota State Fair in Minneapolis, by telling the crowd that this West African proverb was appropriate for the New American of the twentieth century. The truth, which Roosevelt did not realize, was that something like it had appeared in Benjamin Franklin's publication, *Poor Richard's Almanac.*

The "big stick" was of course the needs of a modern navy, which Roosevelt asked his audience to support.

If the American Nation will speak softly, and yet build, and keep at a pitch of the highest training, a thoroughly efficient navy, the Monroe Doctrine will go far. [14]

After describing the needs of a modern navy, Roosevelt then roared his peroration to his audience.

If we have such a navy—if we keep on building it up, we may rest assured that there is but the smallest chance that trouble will ever come to this Nation; and we may likewise rest assured that no foreign power will ever quarrel with us about the Monroe Doctrine. [15]

His updated version of the Monroe Doctrine was a trumpeting manifesto for America's entrance on the world stage. America had come of age and Roosevelt would prove it by sending his "white fleet" around the world. His finishing of the Panama Canal was concrete proof of America's new, powerful political position. No longer did the oceans circumscribe America's foreign policy. America was a new power in world diplomacy, as Roosevelt would show the world when he orchestrated a peace settlement between two warring nations, Russia and Japan, in the Portsmouth, New Hampshire Conference of 1904.

Diplomats assigned to Washington no longer considered it a diplomatic backwater. Americans, too, were becoming more accustomed to Washington's being the center of news.

Roosevelt was the most popular serving president in history, and built a new West Wing onto the Executive Mansion to keep his name in the news. For the first time, press conferences were held and press releases fed daily to reporters. Roosevelt's speeches and photographed appearances were a daily headline feature, and part of the newspapers' new influence in shaping American lives.

But Roosevelt was more than a speaker, he was a cheerleader for what was becoming the world's biggest democracy.

NOTES

1. J.M. Blum, ed., *The Letters of Theodore Roosevelt, Volume 6* (Cambridge, MA: Harvard University Press, 1952), quoted in Humes, *My Fellow Americans,* 104–107.
   2. Ibid.
   3. Ibid.
   4. Ibid.
   5. Ibid.
   6. Ibid.
   7. Ibid.
   8. Ibid.
   9. Ibid.
  10. Ibid.
  11. Ibid.
  12. Ibid.
  13. Ibid.
  14. Ibid.
  15. Ibid.

Chapter Eight

Pacifist Woodrow Wilson Declares War

One of the most quoted lines of President Wilson was to defend American neutrality: "We are too proud to fight."[1] Well, in another way, President Wilson had too much intellectual pride to delegate any writing of speeches to aides.

That was one quality, along with his erudition and zeal for reform, that he shared with his rival Theodore Roosevelt. But in diplomacy, Wilson deemed the Roosevelt approach saber-rattling. The two reform politicians were opposites in personality and style.

If Roosevelt was a warrior and Wilson was a preacher, Wilson resembled a Calvinist cleric who—in the language of the Old Testament prophet— delivered the true gospel to his people. He was a parson's son who found in the mission of American democracy his messianic message.

Wilson entered public life to cleanse the American political temple of corruption. He later stepped into the international arena to inject the democratic idealism of the New World into the corrupt power politics of the Old. He was a latter day Apostle Paul with American democracy as his gospel.

The preacher idealism combined with political realism in Wilson. Yet he was neither the first nor the last American leader to employ righteousness in his rise to power. Still these contradictions in his background made some power brokers uneasy—but he needed their backing to achieve his political goal.

The former president of Princeton and one-time governor of New Jersey liked to portray himself as a Southerner. While a professor, he wrote a biography of George Washington and as president he would cast himself as a continuation of the Virginia Dynasty. But he was hardly a Virginian. His birthplace in Staunton, Virginia, was more an accident of his father's pastoral calling. Woodrow Wilson recast himself as a Southerner to attract Democrats

41

of the old Confederate South. That might explain his reversal of the District of Columbia school integration under Theodore Roosevelt, as well as his refusal to advance anti-lynching laws.

Still, Wilson was a reformer like Roosevelt who inveighed against monopolies and machine politics. His idealism, however, never touched the subject of black subjugation in the South.

Wilson was not actually a bigot even if many black leaders thought he was. But his actions as president reflected the prejudices of his Virginia birthplace. He fired black government appointees of Roosevelt and Taft. Furthermore, he never spoke against state government for its exclusion of blacks in the South.

Wilson never became a popular idol like Theodore Roosevelt, but once the Republican Party split in 1912, Wilson had his opportunity to be the first Democrat since Grover Cleveland to be elected president.

Wilson could never be the exciting personality in the White House like Teddy Roosevelt, but at his first inaugural he proved he could be more eloquent. His brief Inaugural Address struck a spiritual chord. It was that of a preacher, not a politician. A craftsman, he mixed rhyme with repetition and ended with rhetorical challenge. If short, it was one of the most lyrical inaugurals.

> This is not a day of triumph; it is a day of dedication. Here muster, not the forces of party, but the forces of humanity. Men's hearts wait upon us; men's lives hang in the balance; men's hopes call upon us to say what we will do. Who shall live up to the great trust? Who dares fail to try? I summon all men, all patriotic, all forward-looking men, to my side. God helping me, I will not fail them, if they will but counsel and sustain me! [2]

Wilson delivered more inspiring talks than his predecessor. His voice was a resonant baritone, and his looks more handsome with his angular square-jawed face.

The new chief executive who had written as a professor that the president must be like a prime minister put his political thesis into practice. He was the first president to enter the halls of Congress to announce his program. He advanced measures to lower tariffs, enact a stronger Anti-Trust Act, and establish a Federal Reserve. Yet tragedy would darken his administration in the second year of his term. In August 1914, his wife died. In the same month the cataclysm of World War I erupted in Europe.

From the very onset when Imperial Germany invaded neutral Belgium, Wilson's sympathy lay with the Allies. For the present, however, he would adopt a position of official neutrality.

Although the preponderance of American opinion favored the Allies, it did not translate into support for military aid, much less for entry in the War.

Congressmen from the Midwest and West still religiously subscribed to George Washington's doctrine of non-involvement in European affairs.

That neutrality was jolted on May 7, 1915, when the British passenger ship *Lusitania*, carrying over a thousand American passengers, was sunk by a German submarine. Wilson, at first, responded with his ill-chosen phrase, "There is such a thing as a man being too proud to fight."[3]

The tone of his diplomatic protest was stronger. Wilson was worried that the United States might have to take any action necessary to safeguard "its sacred duty of maintaining the rights of the United States and its citizens."[4] William Jennings Bryan, neutralist and isolationist secretary of state, resigned. But his resignation did not impress Theodore Roosevelt. "Wilson and Bryan have quarreled over what seems to me an entirely insignificant point," Roosevelt charged, "that is, as to the percentage of water they shall put into a policy of mere milk and water."[5]

Even within the White House, there was dissent. Colonel House, Wilson's principle aide and personal emissary to the Allies, for example, initially counseled entry into the war.

In the 1916 election, Wilson faced a Republican Party united behind a compromise choice, Supreme Court Justice Charles Evans Hughes—acceptable to both the Taft and Roosevelt wings. Hughes resigned from the court to accept the nomination and run. It would be a close election.

If Wilson did not excite the affections of the country like Teddy Roosevelt, he was more likable than Justice Hughes. Hughes with beard and moustache was regal in appearance and remote to audiences. To them he came off as stiff. On the stump, Wilson, however, was the one-time professor talking to students like his father—a minister addressing his flock.

In simple, direct statements, Wilson's talks were almost sermons. The sins he inveighed against were U-boats, blockades, and the autocrats who wielded them. The resolution he offered was freedom of the seas. Wilson did not disguise his sympathies with Britain and France. But his inclination towards the Allies did not mean intervention.

On May 27 of the election year, 1916, Wilson appeared with Senator Henry Cabot Lodge at a "League to Enforce Peace" meeting to endorse the concept of a League of Nations. It was a plan that—though originally advocated by Roosevelt—had become the personal project of former President Taft. Wilson declared:

> Only when the great nations of the world have reached some sort of agreement as to what they hold to be fundamental to their common interest, and as to some feasible method of acting in concert when any nation or group of nations seeks to disturb those fundamental things, can we feel that civilization is at last in a way of justifying its existence and claiming to be finally established.[6]

Wilson laid down the following principles: national sovereignty, equal rights for small and large nations, and freedom from aggression. He then urged the support of these objectives: a negotiated end to the war, free use of the seas and, significantly, international tribunes.

Although Wilson had been vague about specifics, three days later, he felt it was necessary to calm growing isolationist fears:

> I should never myself, in reference to George Washington's "Farewell Address," consent to an entangling alliance. [7]

Wilson's appeal to both the internationalists and the isolationists worked. In the end, his campaign slogan, "He Kept Us Out of War," was the deciding factor in a tight election. So close was it that the president didn't find out he won until the morning after, when California swung into the Democratic column.

With the election won, Wilson could now afford to spell out the details of the League of Nations and peace settlement package. In an address before the Senate, he offered his five-point plea for mediation: peace without victory; a League of Nations, with American participation in the League; equality between nations; self-determination; and freedom of the seas.

The Germans answered Wilson's peace plan by resuming all-out submarine warfare. Wilson responded by handing the German ambassador his walking papers. For Wilson it was the time of his Garden of Gethsemane. Committing America to war was an awesome and terrible act. He groped for any way to avoid involving America in the European conflict. He tried sending secret peace signals to Germany. He also tried to negotiate secretly with Germany's ally, Austria.

When the time came for his Second Inaugural Address, on March 5, 1917, Wilson spoke of the difficulty in maintaining "calm counsel" in the issue of war and peace. And yet, he could assure his audience:

> The shadows that now lie dark upon our path will soon be dispelled, and we shall walk with the light all about us if we be but true to ourselves. [8]

Like Martin Luther at Worms, Wilson wrestled with his decision. Declaring the war would ensure victory but endanger the post-war peace. Not entering it might be morally correct, but would diminish America's authority on the world stage. Could a mightier justice be achieved through the sin of war?

Wilson, the preacher's son, was well aware of Saint Paul's sermon on Mars Hill in Athens that took Christianity beyond Jerusalem to the world. Wilson, in going to Capitol Hill in Washington, no doubt pictured himself as another evangelist bringing the message of a new political creed to the globe.

The loner Wilson sought his own counsel. He conferred with few except his White House aide, Colonel House, Secretary of War Lindley Garrison, and Secretary of State Robert Lansing, who had replaced Bryan. Then, armed with notes, Wilson began putting his thoughts on paper. Wilson did not have the habit of writing out his speeches word for word. Instead, the law-trained Wilson outlined his points in a logical argument. He would later sound out his thinking to his new wife, Edith Galt, whom he had married on the eve of the previous election.

Wilson drafted the speech first in shorthand and then rewrote it in a mixture of shorthand and longhand. It took him two days, beginning at six in the morning and only taking time out for lunch with his wife. By this time he knew the content like the palm of his hand.

April 2, 1917 was one of those glorious spring days in Washington, D.C. Painted blue skies and billowy clouds capped the Capital City as it awaited the president's appearance.

On the Capitol steps, the scene was far from tranquil, as angry demonstrators made repeated attempts to break through the cordon of policemen who were guarding the entrances. One of the protestors crashed through and assaulted Senator Henry Cabot Lodge. Leader of the pro-war interventionists, the seventy-six year-old Boston Brahmin dispatched the assailant with a right to the jaw. Tensions, even if they didn't run on party lines, were high. Journeying from the White House down Pennsylvania Avenue, Wilson was about to cross the line from the pacifists to the interventionists.

At 8:20 p.m., the president—with his wife, Tumulty his press secretary, and Dr. Grayson, his personal physician—entered the House chamber. He was escorted by a body of cavalry to shield him from the anti-war protestors. On the floor were seated not only congressmen, senators, and members of his cabinet, but also members of the diplomatic corps in evening dress, as well as Supreme Court justices. An expectant hush followed the announcement of the president of the United States.

In a soft baritone, the president opened:

> I have called the Congress into extraordinary session because there are serious, very serious, choices of policy to be made, and made immediately, which it was neither right nor constitutionally permissible that I should assume the responsibility of making.[9]

The president in the role of the righteous prophet then hurled his judgment against the government of the Kaiser.

> The present German submarine warfare against commerce is a warfare against mankind. It is a war against all nations. . . . The challenge is to all mankind. . . . Our motivewill not be revenge or the victorious assertion of the physical might

of the nation, but only the vindication of right, of human right, of which we are only a single champion. [10]

Wilson then discussed and dismissed armed neutrality as "worse than ineffectual;"[11] it was "practically certain to draw us into the war without either the rights or the effectiveness of belligerents." He continued:

> There is but one choice we cannot make, we are incapable of making: we will not choose the path of submission. [12]

As *The New York Times* reported, Congress did not wait to hear the rest of the sentence. At the word "submission" Chief Justice Edward White, who was positioned in the front and center seat, "with an expression of joy and thankfulness on his face, dropped the big, soft hat he had been holding and waived his hands high in the air and brought them together with a bang." The House and Senate followed him with a "roar like a storm," drowning out the rest of Wilson's words: "and suffer the most sacred rights of our Nation and our people to be ignored or violated."[13]

Again, applause erupted when the president in the most formal language called for a declaration of war. Though the wording was dispassionate, his delivery was impassioned.

> With a profound sense of the solemn and even tragical character of the step I am taking and of the grave responsibilities which it involves, but in unhesitating obedience to what I deem my constitutional duty, I advise that Congress declare the recent course of the Imperial German Government to be in fact nothing less than war against the government and people of the United States; that it formally accept the status of belligerent which has thus been thrust upon it, and that it take immediate steps . . . to exert all its power and employ all its resources to bring the government of the German Empire to terms to end the war. [14]

Seldom has a call for a declaration of war been made in such a restrained fashion. No militant words or martial tone attended the president's request. After outlining the preparations for war, Wilson proclaimed the goal of that war: the forces of democracy against autocracy. Like another Apostle, he had preached in his declaration of war his gospel of freedom for the world.

> Our object . . . is to vindicate the principles of peace and justice in the life of the world as against selfish and autocratic power and to set up amongst the really free and self-governed peoples of the world such a concert of purpose and action as will henceforth insure the observance of those principles. [15]

Wilson then made clear that there was "no quarrel with the German people," who were thrust into a conflict "provoked and waged in the interests of dynasties or of little groups of ambitious men who were accustomed to use their fellow men as pawns and tools."[16] Wilson, now looking directly at his audience, raised his voice to that of an evangelist. At this point the cool poise of the diplomat yielded to the passion of a disciple.

> The world must be made safe for democracy.[17]

If it was a sentence Wilson carefully crafted, there was little awareness of this singular statement. One exception was Senator John Williams. Alone, he clapped gravely and emphatically until the rest joined him in a mounting cascade of applause. Wilson paused to continue.

> Its peace must be planted upon the tested foundations of political liberty. We have no selfish ends to serve. We desire no conquest, no dominion. We seek no indemnities for ourselves, no material compensation for the sacrifice we shall freely make. We are but one of the champions of the rights of mankind.[18]

In the righteous language of the apostle Paul, Wilson envisioned the awesome task ahead.

> There are, it may be, many months of fiery trial and sacrifice ahead of us. It is a fearful thing to lead this great peaceful people into war, into the most terrible and disastrous of all wars, civilization itself seeming to be in the balance.[19]

Here Wilson offered his moral justification of the war: a plan to end all future wars by establishing an assembly of free nations. As Luther wrestled with his decision to break from Rome, Wilson had struggled to work out an argument to contravene the sanctified precept of neutrality put down by George Washington.

> But the right is more precious than peace, and we still fight for the things which we have always carried nearest our hearts—for democracy . . . for the rights and liberties of small nations, for a universal dominion of right by such a concert of free people as shall bring peace and safety to all nations and make the world itself at last free.[20]

Wilson was not only preaching the gospel of democracy to the autocrats of Germany and Austria, but also to the Bolsheviks of Russia. The Russian Revolution had erupted in St. Petersburg two months earlier. Czar Nicholas, who had allied his nation with the British and French, had been overthrown by Lenin's Marxists. In a sense, Wilson could be said to be putting the ideals of the American Revolution against those of the Russian Revolution.

Wilson closed with an invocation that began with words from Jefferson's Declaration of Independence and ended with the cry of Martin Luther.

> To such a task we can dedicate our lives and our fortunes, everything that we
> are and everything that we have, with the pride of those who know that the day
> has come when America is privileged to spend her blood and her might for the
> principles that gave her birth and happiness and the peace which she has
> treasured. God helping her, she can do no other. [21]

The Chamber rose, according to *The New York Times*, "in a tumultuous reception with Chief Justice White leading the applause from the front row. Even Henry Cabot Lodge, the most fervent of his critics, went over to shake his hand. Only Senator LaFollette and other mid-western isolationists sat on their hands." [22]

The Chicago Tribune compared Wilson to Lincoln: "The speech was one of the great documents in history." [23] *The Baltimore Sun* said it would go down as "one of the most impressive appeals ever delivered." [24] The poet Alfred Noyes termed the address "the most momentous declaration in the history of the world." [25]

Across the globe, Wilson was hailed as a savior. "By a single statement," wrote *The Philadelphia Inquirer*'s London correspondent, "Wilson has placed himself in the forefront as a world statesman and raised America to a leading place in the Council of Nations." [26] The London *Daily Express* said "his speech was the equal of the Gettysburg Address." [27]

Wilson stood at the summit of his national popularity. Never again would the country stand so united behind him. The problems inherent in mass mobilization would require him to demand powers similar to that of Lincoln. Soon he began to be the target of Republican criticism in the management of the war. Even as the war was ending, in November 1918, Wilson was repudiated by the resurgence of Republican gains in the House and Senate. The professor, in his idealism, had scorned the politicians and now was paying the price of isolation.

Wilson knew how to preach, but not how to politick. Eloquence he could craft but the experience of give and take and compromise he didn't have or try to have.

In his biography of Washington, Wilson noted the General's religious belief that he was the instrument of God to serve and save his country. Both Wilson and Washington adhered to the Doctrine of Providence, that Wilson like Washington was fated to lead this crusade for democracy. "A Messiah complex" may not be a detriment in inspiring a nation, but it is in influencing fellow leaders.

David Lloyd George said of the signing of the Versailles Treaty, "it was like being seated between Jesus Christ and Napoleon." [28] French Prime Minister Georges Clemenceau for his part complained that "Wilson had 14 points where Moses had only 10." [29]

Wilson, who never had surrounded himself with strong personalities, now had to negotiate with Lloyd George and Clemenceau, who were masters of power politics.

His principle of "open covenants openly arrived at"[30] was chimerical idealism never to survive the closed door of diplomatic horse-trading. A weary Wilson returned to America to rally the country around the League.

The battle to win two-thirds of the Republican-controlled Senate for approval was an uphill fight. Perhaps if he had taken ex-President Taft with him to Paris or even had sat down with Senator Lodge and others as he had with Lloyd George and Clemenceau, he would have achieved America's entrance into the League. After all, Lodge was an internationalist who advocated such a tribunal before Wilson. But so intense was his hatred of Lodge that Wilson scorned agreeing to any reservations to the League, no matter how trivial.

On his railway trip through the West, the fatigued Wilson subjected himself to eight or ten speeches a day. He collapsed from an embolism in Pueblo, Colorado, on September 26, 1919. His body, not his will, failed him.

Wilson lived out his presidency as a partially paralyzed wreck. His endeavor to make the United States a member of the League of Nations was in vain.

If Wilson became a martyr to the cause of internationalism, it was himself as much as his opponents who shaped that fate. In him burned not only the moral principles of the prophet, but the overwhelming pride. The vision of the preacher was undone by the pride of one who would not stoop to ply the politician's craft.

In his declaration of war, Wilson tapped the roots of American idealism to preach democracy as a gospel for the world. He failed to see that this stubborn faith could be as insular as the isolationists he fought.

Eloquent idealism is not enough for the great statesman if he lacks the political skills to implement it.

NOTES

1. Woodrow Wilson, "Address to Naturalized Citizens at Convention Hall, Philadelphia" (May 10, 1915), John T. Woolley and Gerhard Peters, eds., *The American Presidency Project, University of California, Santa Barbara,* accessed August 28, 2015, http://www.presidency.ucsb.edu/ws/?pid=65388.

2. Woodrow Wilson, Wilson's First Inaugural Address, Washington, D.C., March 4, 1913, quoted in Humes, *My Fellow Americans,* 114.

3. Wilson, "Address to Naturalized Citizens at Convention Hall, Philadelphia," *The American Presidency Project,* accessed August 28, 2015, http://www.presidency.ucsb.edu/ws/?pid=65388.

4. Woodrow Wilson, "U.S. Protest over the Sinking of the Lusitania" (May 13, 1915), *The Lusitania Resource,* accessed August 28, 2015, http://www.rmslusitania.info/primary-docs/wilson-notes/us-protest-1/.

5. Theodore Roosevelt, letter to Oscar King Davis, June 23, 1915, quoted in Humes, *My Fellow Americans,* 115.

6. Humes, *My Fellow Americans,* 116.

7. Ibid.

8. Woodrow Wilson, Wilson's Second Inaugural Address, Washington, D.C., March 5, 1917, quoted in Humes, *My Fellow Americans,* 116.

9. Woodrow Wilson, Address to Joint Session of Congress, April 2, 1917, quoted in Humes, *My Fellow Americans,* 118.

10. Ibid.

11. Ibid.

12. Ibid.

13. Ibid., 118–119.

14. Ibid., 119.

15. Ibid.

16. Ibid.

17. Ibid.

18. Ibid.

19. Ibid., 126.

20. Ibid.

21. Ibid.

22. Ibid.

23. Ibid., 121.

24. Ibid.

25. Ibid.

26. Ibid.

27. Ibid.

28. Ibid.

29. Ibid.

30. Ibid., 122.

Chapter Nine

Warren Harding Revisited

Ever since H.L. Menken, the acid-wit critic of the "Roaring Twenties," the Left's spin on Warren Harding has been that he was "the best looking and worst performing American president in history." True, if his square-jawed chiseled looks were the only criterion for Mount Rushmore, Harding might have made a handsome addition to the presidential pinnacle. But to glibly dismiss him as the worst is to slight some of his achievements.

For one thing, it could be argued that the one-time Ohio senator selected the most star-studded cabinet in U.S. history. For secretary of state he chose Charles Evans Hughes. The distinguished Hughes, who had barely lost the presidency to Woodrow Wilson, had resigned from the bench in 1916 to be the Republican nominee. Earlier, Hughes had been the governor of New York State, the largest state in the Union.

Despite the opposition from Senator Henry Cabot Lodge, Harding managed to outmaneuver Lodge to give Hughes the senior cabinet position. The country wholeheartedly approved of the selection.

For Treasury, Harding chose the most respected financier in the world—Andrew Mellon. The billionaire banker's fortune was only exceeded by Rockefeller's. The Pittsburgh titan in steel and railroads was no "robber baron" like some of his contemporary corporate titans. He was a philanthropist whose gifts established the National Gallery of Art. Mellon was deemed to be the ablest secretary of the treasury since Alexander Hamilton.

Usually, cabinet secretaries gain distinction from the office they occupy. Few add eminence to the position the way Herbert Hoover did. Harding had persuaded him to become secretary of commerce. Esteemed as a world statesman, Hoover had won a Nobel Prize for his food relief of Europe in World War I. The millionaire engineer had established a world relief organization that was later adopted by the UN. He was the "dream" presidential candidate mentioned by the press and members of both parties. As the new Secretary of Commerce, Hoover was widely acclaimed by the press and both parties.

All of these cabinet selections were announced before the March inauguration. But perhaps Harding's most applauded selection was his nomination of former President Taft to be chief justice. After his defeat in 1912, Taft had become dean of Yale Law School. Harding's selection of his fellow Ohioan to be chief justice was a masterstroke. For a former president to preside over the court brought a new esteem and distinction to the Third Branch of Government. The choice won acclaim not only from the organized bar, but from both parties as well as the press. Similarly, Harding was the first president to establish a Bureau of the Budget, which succeeded in cutting government expenditures by $1 billion.

Internationally, the great achievement of the Harding administration was a naval disarmament treaty that reversed the direction of Wilson. When the Harding administration cut back arms, it forced Britain and Japan to join the reduction in naval fleets. To meet the proposed goal, the United States had to scrap ships amounting to 480,000 tons. The conference produced monumental results. By February 1922, the participants had come to eight agreements limiting the use of poison gas, and a working resolution of tariff issues that would strengthen the "open door" policy in China. Harding was widely praised for the accomplishments of the disarmament conference. By persuasion of his former Senate colleagues, Harding managed to get almost everything that he needed from the Senate.

On December 8, 1922, Harding would deliver his second and last State of the Union message. In it he called for the end of child labor—by Constitutional Amendment, if necessary.

Harding was also the first president to reach out to black voters. In a special message to Congress in 1922, Harding called for anti-lynching laws. A bill was passed in the House, but stopped in the Senate by filibustering Southern Democrats.

Harding also appointed blacks to high-level posts in the Departments of Labor and Interior, and appointed a black Minister to Portugal. Harding was also the first president to journey south to speak about civil rights. He said it was time for political and economic equality of the races. To an integrated audience, he declared, "Whether you like it or not, unless our democracy is a lie, you must stand for that equality."[1]

This was not the speech of a reactionary Republican, but of a Progressive. Similarly, Harding brooked attacks from Democrats when he urged the pardon of Socialist Eugene Debs, who had been jailed for sedition by the Wilson administration. After the war ended, Wilson's own attorney general, Mitchell Palmer, had urged Wilson to pardon Debs. Wilson, however, denied that petition. Progressives such as Clarence Darrow and Upton Sinclair, as well as Britons George Bernard Shaw and H.G. Wells, also endorsed the Harding pardon.

But history has painted the prejudiced Wilson as a progressive and Harding as a know-nothing reactionary. Certainly Harding had not the scholarly credentials of a Wilson. Few presidents had. But neither was he the dim-witted stooge that H.L. Menken described.

Though Harding had nothing to do with the Teapot Dome scandal that emerged in his last year, he is still tarnished with it. At his unexpected death in the spring of 1923, the country mourned him—but not for long, as the stench from the oil leases negotiated by his secretary of the interior, Albert Fall, permeated Washington. No one has ever tied Teapot Dome to Harding, but it did stain his reputation.

To historians, a crusading visionary endeavoring to erect a world organization that would prevent future wars was succeeded by an ordinary run-of-the-mill politician. A global missionary for peace was succeeded by a political mediocrity. Never mind that the practical politician Harding would do more in the international arena to limit war by his naval disarmament treaty with the global military powers at that time—the United States, Britain, and Japan.

Whatever Harding's limitations as president, he harbored no prejudices as had his predecessor Wilson, who governed as a Virginia Democrat and who held some biases towards black Americans that reflected the Southern wing of his party. Wilson had dismissed blacks who had been appointed to government posts under William Howard Taft and Theodore Roosevelt. During the Wilson administration, integration of public schools in the District of Columbia was halted. Segregation was also imposed in the armed forces.

Conversely, Harding was the first president to address a Southern and integrated audience on the need for civil rights and educational opportunity for Southern blacks. Again the practical politician, Harding displayed more intellectual courage than the previous president, who had proclaimed such noble ideals to the world.

Yet the academics and pundits sighted no progressiveness in the Ohio politician. Much the way the intellectual community originally saw Harry Truman, who succeeded the mythic President Roosevelt in 1945, they saw a run-of-the mill politician following the champion against tyranny. Not until he won election against Dewey in 1948 did the world statesman of the Marshall Plan, the Truman Doctrine, and champion of the United Nation's principles against the invasion of South Korea emerge.

The intellectual community saw no such potential for statesmanship in Harding. His alliterative summons in Boston in 1920 when he stated: "America's present need is not heroics, but healings; not nostrums, but normalcy; not revolution, but restoration. . . ."[2] struck a popular resonance with the public if mocked by punditry.

Similarly, his Inaugural Address was denounced by the academic left. Judson Welliver, who under the title of "literary clerk" became the first White House speechwriter, considered it a failure. The new president declared:

> Standing in this presence, mindful of the solemnity of this occasion . . . I must utter my belief in the divine inspiration of the Founding Fathers. Surely there must have been God's intent in the making of this New-World Republic. [. . .] The recorded progress of our Republic, materially and spiritually, in itself proves the wisdom of the inherited policy of noninvolvement in Old World affairs.[3]

Harding then renounced involvement in Europe:

> . . . we seek no part in directing the destinies of the Old World. We do not mean to be entangled. We will accept no responsibility except as our own conscience and judgment, in each instance, may determine. [. . .] We can reduce the abnormal expenditures, and we will. We can strike at war taxation, and we must. [. . .] We contemplate the immediate task of putting our public household in order. We need a rigid and yet sane economy. . . . we must strive for normalcy to reach stability.[4]

Then Harding called for ways to achieve normalcy: administrative efficiency; lightening the tax burden; following sound commercial practices; and eliminating unnecessary interference of government with business. Next, he introduced a new dimension to inaugural addresses. For the first time, a president designates women as a political cause:

> With the nationwide introduction of womanhood into our political life, we may count upon her intuitions, her refinements, her intelligence, and her influence to exalt the social order. We count upon her exercise of the full privileges and the performance of the duties of citizenship to speed the attainment of the highest state.[5]

Harding then praises free enterprise:

> Wealth is not inimical to welfare; it ought to be its friendliest agency. There never can be equality of rewards or possessions so long as the human plan contains varied talents and differing degrees of industry and thrift, but ours ought to be a country free from the great blotches of distressed poverty. We ought to find a way to guard against the perils and penalties of unemployment. We want an America of homes, illumined with hope and happiness, where mothers . . . may preside as befits the hearthstone of American citizenship.[6]

Harding then went into the banalities that caused intellectual critics to squirm:

Service is the supreme commitment of life. I would rejoice to acclaim the era of the Golden Rule and crown it with the autocracy of service. [7]

Harding closes with the scriptural line used by other presidents:

"What does the Lord require of thee but to do justly, and to love mercy, and to walk humbly with thy God?" This I plight to God and country. [8]

If Harding's Inaugural expressed not the eloquence of a Jefferson or Lincoln before him, nor later in FDR, JFK, or Ronald Reagan, neither does it deserve the scorn of H.L. Menken or even Harding's later speechwriter, Judson Welliver. It was an accurate mirroring of an America weary of grandiose appeals to world peace and justice.

NOTES

1. Warren Harding, Address in Woodrow Wilson Park, Birmingham, Alabama, October 26, 1921, quoted in John W. Dean, *Warren Harding: The American Presidents Series* (New York: Times Books, Henry Holt and Company, 2004), 126.

2. Warren Harding, Campaign Address in Boston, 1920, quoted in Dean, *Warren Harding*, 57.

3. Robert V. Remini and Terry Golway, eds., *Fellow Citizens: The Penguin Book of U.S. Presidential Inaugural Addresses* (New York: Penguin Books, 2008), 298.

4. Ibid., 302.

5. Ibid., 303.

6. Ibid., 304.

7. Ibid., 305.

8. Ibid.

Chapter Ten

Calvin Coolidge,
Philosopher from Vermont

To contemporary Americans of his day, the thirtieth president was portrayed as either dull or droll. Dorothy Parker, whose husband Sinclair Lewis would satirize the American middle class in his novels, joked when he died in 1933, "How could they tell?" Compared to the charismatic Harding, who preceded him until his unexpected death, the new president's sour looks made Alice Roosevelt Longworth comment, "He looked as if he was weaned on a pickle." If there was in his personality a touch of the comic, it was due to his Yankee brevity, which was iconic.

When a Washington dowager told Coolidge she had boasted to her husband that she could get the president to say more than two words, "Silent Cal" replied, "You lose."

Another time, a Washington reporter asked Coolidge, "What was the subject of the minister's sermon you just heard?" "Sin," was Coolidge's one-word answer. "What did he say about it?" the journalist queried further. "He was agin it," replied Coolidge.

To the self-appointed literati of the patronizing Left—exemplified by the Algonquin Club Round Table, which included Nobel Prize winner Sinclair Lewis and his wife Dorothy Parker—Coolidge was the personification of H.L. Menken's boobocracy, the unlettered philistines of majoritarian America. Their Pecksniffian contempt would continue from FDR to JFK.

For all the intellectual vaunting of Jacqueline Kennedy for bringing the arts to Washington, it was Grace Goodhue Coolidge who brought the symphony to our nation's capital. Jack Kennedy's cultural preferences ranged from mysteries like James Bond to musical comedies like *South Pacific,* while Coolidge attended music recitals and read Milton's "Paradise Lost."

For recreation on his honeymoon, Coolidge translated Dante's "Inferno" from medieval Latin into English.

President Reagan, to the Washington press corps' sniggering, restored Coolidge's portrait to a place of prominence in the White House next to those of Washington and Lincoln. Reagan appreciated that Silent Cal stood for budget cutting, tax reform, and the efficacy of limited government. He was, in Amity Shlaes' splendid phrase, "our great refrainer," the precise opposite of FDR and LBJ. He abstained from grand-sounding programs that cost money with few results to show for it. He didn't believe in padding programs or padding his word. Coolidge reduced the national debt from $28 billion to $18 billion. He outdid Reagan.

George W. Crane, an excellent writer who wrote speeches for Coolidge, was like him—terse and to the point. Today's speechwriters could learn from him.

In fact, it was Coolidge's terseness that would make him president, with a single well-crafted sentence. As governor of Massachusetts, he had to confront the Boston police strike of 1919. When the majority of the Boston police went on strike, lawlessness erupted in the city. Coolidge ordered the striking policemen fired and called in the state militia to patrol the streets and keep order.

Coolidge declared, "There is no right to strike against the public safety by anybody, anywhere, any time."[1] Coolidge was suddenly a national figure, and the Republican Party, to balance the charming, talkative, and lackadaisical Harding, selected Coolidge as his running mate. Coolidge was a natural.

The invitation to speak at the Sesquicentennial in Philadelphia he felt by command, by destiny, to accept. He was the only president to be born on the Fourth of July. As one who now found himself by God's providence to be president, he felt called upon to deliver a message that transcended the usual patriotic sentiments.

For preparation, Coolidge turned to his fellow New Englanders Daniel Webster and Ralph Waldo Emerson. Webster had spoken at Bunker Hill in 1825 on the fiftieth anniversary of the battle, and Emerson at Concord Bridge at the centennial of that battle, in 1875.

Coolidge saw America in the full flush of prosperity, enjoying the fruits of freedom, but forgetting the faith in God that inspired those resolves of freedom.

As the cherry blossoms imparted their pink glow to the Washington spring, Coolidge pored over the words of Puritan preachers. He arrived at the conclusion that the drive for independence owed more to the Puritan theologians than the Enlightenment intellectuals. To Coolidge, the sources to study were not the natural law philosophers like John Locke and David Hume, who inspired Jefferson, but Puritan divines such as Thomas Hooker and John Wise. For Coolidge, whose first name announced his Protestant heritage, the eighteenth-century British philosophers may have given color to our found-ers' thought, but Puritan theologians had given the substance of their creed and conviction—the warp and woof of their background and beliefs.

On his upstairs desk lay neat piles of extracts from selected sermons provided by the Library of Congress. In his tiny scrawl, Coolidge penned the first draft of his address on yellow legal tablets. The draft was then typed by his secretary.

Coolidge relied on neither a research assistant nor a literary clerk. He had dismissed Judson Welliver, Harding's speechwriter—the first to be em-ployed solely for that purpose—eighteen months before.

On July 4, 1926, Coolidge awakened to find his fifty-fourth birthday rained upon. The next day, President and Mrs. Coolidge, along with Attorney General John Sargent, drove to Union Station and caught the morning train to Philadelphia. More than 200 souls had braved the rain to greet the president.

At Memorial Stadium, he was introduced by Mayor Kendrick. Coolidge had entitled his address, "The Inspiration of the Declaration." It was more a lecture than rhetoric and more sermon than speech.

Coolidge opened by declaring:

> At the end of 150 years the four corners of the earth unite in coming to Philadelphia as to a holy shrine in grateful acknowledgment of a service so great, which a few inspired men have rendered to humanity, that is still the pre-eminent support of free government throughout the world.[2]

In this sentence, Coolidge affirmed what Lincoln first said at Gettysburg and Wilson later expanded during World War I—that America has a spiritual vocation as the first democracy. Almost a generation before the end of World War II, Coolidge was speaking of America's role as a leader of the free world.

Continuing, he reinforced this idea of a holy mission:

> It is little wonder that people at home and abroad consider Independence Hall as hallowed ground and revere the Liberty Bell as a sacred relic. That pile of bricks and mortar, that mass of metal, might appear to the uninstructed as only the outgrown meeting place and the shattered bell of a former time, useless now because of more modern conveniences, but [. . .] they are the framework of a spiritual event.[3]

The event was "The Declaration of Independence." It represented an up-rising of the people.

It was not, of course, a movement that came to us from the top. To Coolidge, this was a central point. An outsider amid the rich and sophisticat-ed at Amherst College, Coolidge took pride in his own descent from the yeomanry stock of Yankee farmers. It was these sturdy and humble folks who strove for independence, not the aristocracy whose position during the war was an attitude of utter neutrality or open hostility.

> The American Revolution represented the informed and mature convictions of a great mass of independent, liberty-loving, God-fearing people who knew their rights, and possessed the courage to maintain them. [4]

But Coolidge added that our forefathers fought for more than independence.

> There is something beyond the establishment of a new nation, great as that event would be, in the Declaration of Independence which has ever since caused it to be regarded as one of the great charters that not only was to liberate America but was everywhere to ennoble humanity. [5]

Coolidge then re-states the central theme of his address:

> It was not because it was proposed to establish a new nation, but because it was proposed to establish a nation on new principles, that July 4, 1776, has come to be regarded as one of the greatest days in history. [6]

These principles, stated Coolidge, were that "all men are created equal" and that "they are endowed with certain inalienable rights" and therefore that the source of the just powers of government must be derived from the consent of the people.

Like many past American orators, Coolidge restated the familiar Jefferson thesis. But then he shed the role of politician for professor. He lectured his audience that the principle that sovereignty must rest with the people was not really a new idea. What was revolutionary was that "all men are created equal."

> The idea that the people have a right to choose their own rulers was not new in political history. It was the foundation of every attempt to dispose of an unpopular king. But we should search these documents in vain for an assertion of equality. That principle had not appeared before as a declaration of any nation. It was profoundly revolutionary. It is one of the cornerstones of American institutions. [7]

Coolidge then traced the development of the doctrine by New England's Puritan clergy. He cited first the Reverend Thomas Hooker's 1638 sermon to the General Court. Next, he cited the Reverend John Wise, the leader of the 1687 revolt against Edmund Andros, the royal governor of Massachusetts, and such eloquent preachers as Jonathan Edwards and George Whitfield.

They preached equality because they believed in the fatherhood of God and the brotherhood of man. They justified freedom by the text that we are all created in the divine image, all partakers of the divine spirit. [8]

These Puritans believed that authority came only from God. If kings did not have divine right, men must have the political right to choose their own governments.

Placing every man on a plane where he acknowledged no superiors, where no one possessed any right to rule over him, he must inevitably choose his own rulers through a system of self-government. . . . These great truths were in the air that our people breathed. Whatever else we may say of it, the Declaration of Independence was profoundly American [9]

The rain-drenched crowds began to applaud the last line, but without a pause, Coolidge uttered a stern reminder to those enjoying the fruits of an unprecedented prosperity.

In its main features the Declaration of Independence is a great spiritual document. It is a declaration not of material but of spiritual conceptions. Equality, liberty, popular sovereignty, the rights of man . . . they have their source and their roots in religious convictions. [. . .] Unless the faith of the American people in these religious convictions is to endure, the principles of our Declaration will perish. We cannot continue to enjoy the result if we neglect and abandon the cause. [10]

Then in an aphoristic parallelism, Coolidge compared the difference between the American Revolution and the recent Communist one in Russia headed by Comrade Lenin.

Governments do not make ideals, but ideals make governments. [11]

The government, Coolidge contended, cannot dictate ideals, for that responsibility rests with the people.

There is no method by which that burden can be shifted to the government. It is not the enactment, but the observance of laws, that creates the character of a nation. [12]

Some in the audience thought they heard an allusion to "Teapot Dome." Coolidge continued:

Ours is a government of the people. It represents their will. Its officers may sometimes go astray, but that is not a reason for criticizing the principles of our institutions. The real heart of the American Government depends upon the heart of the people. [13]

Coolidge then sought to remind his audience that the Founding Fathers were men of deep spiritual conviction. He closed, as he began, as a preacher to those who had made their pilgrimage to a national shrine. His sermon was an implicit contrast between the American and Russian revolutions. If theirs was based on the material in life, ours was based on the spiritual.

> We live in an age of science and of abounding accumulation of material things. These did not create our Declaration. Our Declaration created them. The things of the spirit come first. Unless we cling to that, all our material prosperity, overwhelming though it may appear, will turn to a barren scepter in our grasp. If we are to maintain the great heritage which has been bequeathed to us, we must be like-minded as the fathers who created it. We must not sink into a pagan materialism. [. . .] We must follow the spiritual and moral leadership which they showed.[14]

The wet, weary audience applauded mostly out of respect for the president and relief at his conclusion. Coolidge had been more expository than eloquent. He had drilled into them like a professor that the idea of equality originated not with eighteenth-century philosophers, but rather with seventeenth-century preachers.

And he exhorted them not to let material benefits make them forget their spiritual debts. It was not the first nor last time a president would deliver a spiritual warning. The professorial Woodrow Wilson and born-again Jimmy Carter come to mind. The best comparison may be with the Eisenhower Farewell Address.

Coolidge wrote like he governed. No superfluous adjective embroidered his prose; neither did the use of the possessive voice enervate his purpose and intent. Perhaps Coolidge lacked the foresight of a prophet, but this son of a New England Town Meeting president did possess faith in the American democracy.

If he was no visionary, he was an idealist and his compass was the Constitution. Oddly, this frugal Yankee amid an expansive era was a man to fit his time. He did not glorify himself or the presidency. But in the 1926 Fourth of July celebration, he did exalt the ideals that made his country great.

NOTES

1. Humes, *My Fellow Americans,* 131.
2. Ibid., 130.
3. Ibid., 139.
4. Ibid., 140.
5. Ibid.
6. Ibid.
7. Ibid.
8. Ibid.
9. Ibid., 141.

10. Ibid.
11. Ibid.
12. Ibid.
13. Ibid., 141.
14. Ibid., 142.

Chapter Eleven

FDR—Recovery in Peace and Victory in War

Franklin Delano Roosevelt was more than a president—he was a presence. His reassuring patrician tones were a familiar voice during the Depression and then in World War II. He was the first president to project his personality into the family living room. If radio became in those years the focal center-piece of furniture, Roosevelt more than any commentator or entertainer commanded its airwaves. His Fireside Chats were models of conversational intimacy. They evoked a credibility lacking in the frenetic cant and histrionic excesses of the typical politicians heard at a courthouse rally. Roosevelt seemed more real to them. In the despair of the Thirties, he offered hope. When World War II erupted with the bombing of Pearl Harbor, Roosevelt would manifest the resolve that promised victory.

Like his distant cousin Theodore Roosevelt, Franklin Roosevelt understood that politics was theater. And FDR was better at it than TR. True, the second Roosevelt had the advantage of radio, which the first Roosevelt did not. But the microphone notwithstanding, FDR had other assets his cousin lacked. His was a patrician face that wasn't a caricature, as was TR's with its prominent teeth, pince-nez spectacles, and bushy moustache. Franklin Roosevelt also had a commanding voice that didn't have to roar to invite attention.

The Hyde Park Roosevelt was the natural actor that his more direct-spoken Oyster Bay cousin was not. FDR could play a range of emotional moods: compassion, anger, resolve and humor. He also had the actor's art of timing, pause, and variance of tone to deliver a line and sentence.

Yet it must be stated that without Theodore Roosevelt, there wouldn't have been a Franklin Roosevelt. The younger Roosevelt had idolized his presidential cousin. Franklin's wooing of TR's niece was no accident. Some wondered what the tall and fine-featured Roosevelt saw in the shy and awkward Eleanor. His surname and kinship to the president helped unseat a Republican in a state senate race. Yet despite his cousinly connection, he backed Woodrow Wilson in the three-way race that doomed the Republicans. From President-Elect Wilson, he sought the assistant secretary of the Navy appointment that the older Roosevelt had made newsworthy under McKinley. Finally, as one whose only elective position had been that of a state senator, he would not have been selected as vice president under James Cox in 1920. It was his last name that put him on the ticket in 1920, an uphill race that looked like a sure Republican victory. But taking a page from Theodore Roosevelt's book, Franklin hired a train to do a thousand-speech tour to every part of the country. Without the hundreds and hundreds of Democratic leaders that he met in this thirty-state campaign, he would not have had his political base to mount a presidential campaign twelve years later.

That is not to suggest that Franklin Roosevelt had an easy path to the White House. The polio he incurred at Campobello in 1921 would have ended the presidential ambitions of any average politician. His mother, Sara Delano, thought it was God's way of telling him to retire and live the life of a country squire at Hyde Park. Roosevelt's chain-smoking and hard-drinking friend, Louis Howe, personified everything unsavory FDR's mother detested about the dirty game of politics. Howe, who had picked Roosevelt as his political star, did not want him to quit politics. Neither did his wife, Eleanor, who couldn't see herself playing nurse to a cripple for the rest of her life. Her inexhaustible energy had under Howe's tutelage been directed into women's causes. By 1921 she had become a personality in her own right.

Roosevelt did learn to stand with braces and move about with assistance, but Louis Howe became his legs for his continuing involvement in public life. Though Roosevelt restricted himself to public ceremonies where his presence was demanded, he kept his name alive to Democrats by another communication invention of the twentieth century . . . the telephone. It would be as important to him as the radio would be a decade later. The phone allowed him to use his hearty distinctive voice to keep in contact with the political friends he had gained in the 1920 campaign for vice president.

The opportunity to address all those Democratic politicians came in 1924. New York Governor Al Smith was running for president. Smith, a Catholic, needed a distinguished Protestant name to nominate him. Judge Joseph Proskauer, who was Smith's answer to Roosevelt's wordsmith Sam Rosenman, drafted a speech for Roosevelt with the quotation of "The Happy Warrior." It was rejected by Roosevelt as "too precious" for the ears of the delegates. According to Proskauer's grandson, Tony Smith (the author's roommate at Williams College), Proskauer insisted on it; Roosevelt would later take credit for the phrase and deny that it came from Proskauer.

Yet for Roosevelt it was not the speech but getting to the podium to make the address that proved challenging. He couldn't allow those delegates to see him in a wheelchair. He arrived at Madison Square Garden early before most of the crowd had arrived. There, with his two sons Jimmy and Elliott flanking him, he swung himself forward by crutches, with a bevy of young Democratic women following in their trail to mask FDR's halting progress to the platform. When his name was called, Roosevelt propelled himself and grabbed the edge of the speaker's stand. For minutes he tried to capture his breath as the delegates stood and applauded their vice presidential nominee from four years before. Roosevelt closed with this paragraph:

> He has the power to strike at error and wrongdoing that makes his adversaries quail before him. He has a personality that carries to every hearer not only the sincerity, but the righteousness of his ways. He is "The Happy Warrior" of the political battlefield—Alfred E. Smith. [1]

Young Roosevelt was the most popular figure at the 1924 convention, but Smith would lose to John W. Davis, a Wall Street lawyer originally from West Virginia. President Calvin Coolidge would then overwhelm Davis in the election.

In 1928, Governor Smith would win the nomination. But this time Smith would be pitted against Herbert Hoover, the humanitarian hero of post-war relief in Europe.

In 1928, the "Roaring Twenties" were at their peak. The Catholic Governor from New York was the underdog pitted against Hoover. To have a chance, Smith needed New York to stay in the Democratic column.

Again, Smith turned to Roosevelt, who demurred. He gave as his reason his crippled legs. Smith thundered back, "Frank, you don't have to be an acrobat to be governor." Smith turned to the reluctant Roosevelt's wife, Eleanor. She called her husband at Warm Springs, his new favorite vacation resort, and he agreed.

Roosevelt won the state of New York, but Smith lost the nation. The economic bubble had burst in 1929 and suddenly the governor of the biggest state in the Union had the inside track to defeat the hapless Hoover, who was mired in the Depression. In a radio address written for FDR by Raymond Moley, a Columbia University professor and one of FDR's braintrusters, Moley used as a theme "the forgettable man at the bottom of the economic pyramid, the forgotten man," which came from a speech given by Social Darwinist William Graham Sumner of Yale University in 1883.

With his flair for the dramatic, Governor Roosevelt flew by airplane from Albany to Chicago for the nomination. There he first read lines from Louis Howe's draft, which he hadn't read over, but then switched to Ray Moley's when he noticed Moley's puzzled frown:

> Ours must be a party of liberal thought, of planned action, of enlightened international outlook, and of the greatest good to the greatest number of citizens.[2]

Roosevelt then asked:

> What do the people of America want more than anything else? [. . .] Work and security—these are more than words.[3]

In mellifluous tones, he then delivered his clarion promise:

> I pledge you, I pledge myself, to a new deal for the American people.[4]

The "New Deal" might not have become the catchword of the Roosevelt administration but for Herbert Bayard Swope, editor of *The New York World.* He wrote a tract two days after Roosevelt's speech that alluded to FDR's cousin Teddy's use of "Square Deal," with references to Mark Twain's use of it in *A Connecticut Yankee in King Arthur's Court.* (Second to Twain, FDR is the most cited American in *Bartlett's Quotations.*)

The phrase brought the convention to its feet. That cavalier attention to the speech, which Roosevelt with his usual aplomb delivered without a hitch, reinforced the view at that time that Roosevelt was a playboy in politics. Journalist and political commentator Walter Lippmann described him as "a pleasant man who, without any important qualifications for the office, would very much like to be President."[5]

It is true that FDR didn't have the mind of his cousin Theodore. He hadn't been Phi Beta Kappa at Harvard and he hadn't read thousands of books, but he did share his love of center stage, and theatrics.

The Thirties were the moment in which movies really became America's entertainment. Just as Hollywood would hire scores of screenwriters, Roosevelt would sign on many speechwriters.

In an orchestra, different instruments can signal different chords of emotion: strings for compassion, trumpets for summons to action, the bassoon for a mock epic. Roosevelt had a good ear as well as eye for the ringing catchphrase or slogan.

He was no stranger to writing. He had been editor of *The Harvard Crimson* and was known for his crafting of arresting headlines. He later said that advertising was the field that attracted him most if he hadn't chosen politics.

In his 1933 Inaugural Address, Roosevelt's speechwriter Judge Sam Rosenman helped him come up with one of the most memorable lines in the history of presidential addresses. Roosevelt opened in a ringing voice:

> This is a day of national consecration.[6]

As millions huddled around radio sets, Roosevelt then issued his trumpet call:

> So, first of all, let me assert my firm belief that the only thing we have to fear is fear itself—nameless, unreasoning, unjustified terror which paralyzes needed efforts to convert retreat into advance.[7]

Rosenman's first words for Roosevelt were a prefatory device once used by Pericles to underline what came next. It was a line borrowed from Henry David Thoreau, with the repetition of "fear." It reassured Americans as no sentence ever had.

Later Roosevelt would employ two biblical allusions from Proverbs and Matthew that denounced Wall Street and Big Business:

> They have no vision, and when there is no vision the people perish. Yes, the money changers have fled from their high seats in the temple of our civilization.[8]

Roosevelt outlined the need for "strict supervision of all banking and credits and investment . . . an end to speculation with other people's money." Congress must also provide for "an adequate but sound currency." Then, in an untypically grim tone for Roosevelt, he directed a challenge to Congress:

> But, in the event that the Congress shall fail to take one of these two courses . . . I shall ask the Congress for the one remaining instrument to meet the crisis—broad Executive power to wage war against the emergency, as great as the power that would be given to me if we were in fact invaded by a common foe.[9]

In that dire moment the people wanted action and the new president gave it to them in one hundred days' legislation. FDR's first Executive Order was the Bank Holiday. It was issued a little more than a week after his inaugural. He wanted to spell out the need for action.

Raymond Moley, who would write the president's remarks, called the various radio stations. He explained that the tone of the talk would be informal and conversational. Robert Trout, the Washington Bureau Chief for CBS, announced before it, "The president wants to come to your home and sit at your fireside for a Fireside Chat." Roosevelt loved the phrase and would deliver "a Fireside Chat" fourteen times in 1933 and twenty-seven times altogether during his presidency.

> My friends, I want to talk for a few minutes with the people of the United States about banking. . . .[10]

The president explained that because too many worried depositors had withdrawn money:

> We had a bad banking situation. Some of our bankers had shown themselves either incompetent or dishonest in their handling of the people's funds. [. . .] I do not promise you that every bank will be reopened or that individual losses will not be suffered, but there will be no losses that possibly could be avoided; and there would have been more and greater losses had we continued to drift. [11]

He closed:

> You people must have faith; you must not be stampeded by rumors or guesses. Let us unite in banishing fear. We have provided the machinery to restore our financial system; it is up to you to support and make it work. It is your problem no less than it is mine. Together we cannot fail. [12]

Surprisingly, the Democrats would break all historical precedent and pick up seats in the off-year election of 1934. It was a signal for FDR to move more left on social and business issues. Speechwriter Raymond Moley would quit in protest.

More significantly, Al Smith—the Democratic Party candidate in 1928— would address a white-tie dinner at the Mayflower Hotel in Washington and assail the Roosevelt record to an audience packed with DuPonts, Mellons, and Vanderbilts. Smith obliquely accused Roosevelt of fouling America's pure, free air with the smell of Bolshevism.

The attendance of the various kings and princes of American aristocracy gave the opportunity for new speechwriter Stanley High to play the class card in a speech for FDR attacking the "royalists," on June 27, 1936 at the Democratic Convention in Philadelphia. High was a former journalist whom Rosenman identified as the top phrasemaker of the speechwriting staff.

> Liberty requires opportunity to make a living [...] a living which gives a man not only enough to live by, but something to live for. For too many of us, the political equality we once had is meaningless in the face of economic inequality. A small group has concentrated into their own hands almost complete control of other people's property, other people's money, other people's lives. These economic royalists complain that we seek to overthrow the institutions of America. What they really complain of is that we seek to take away their power. In vain they seek to hide behind the flag and the Constitution. [13]

Roosevelt's voice rose and fell as he lifted the audience through the rhythmic cadence:

Governments can err. Presidents do make mistakes. But the immortal Dante tells us that divine justice weighs the sins of the cold-blooded and the sins of the warm-hearted on different scales. Better the occasional faults of a Government that lives in a spirit of charity than the consistent omissions of a Government frozen in the ice of its own indifference. [14]

The Convention stood with another roaring ovation. When it stilled, Roosevelt lowered his voice to issue his call to action:

There is a mysterious cycle in human events. To some generations much is given. Of other generations much is asked. This generation of Americans has a rendezvous with destiny. [15]

This last line is from the Second Inaugural. It is perhaps the most quoted of lines, particularly in high school commencement addresses.

Thomas (Tommy the Cork) Corcoran was a lawyer, not a speechwriter. He told the author that he had advised Raymond Moley that if the theme of the First Inaugural was "relief," the Second Inaugural had to be about "change" and "the call to citizenry to bring about such change." Corcoran recited to the author the poem by World War I poet Alan Seeger. It begins: "I have a rendezvous with death/At some disputed barricade. . . ." Corcoran changed "death" to "destiny" and suggested it to FDR, who passed it on to Rosenman.

Roosevelt scored a landslide victory over Governor Alf Landon of Kansas, carrying forty-six states. The huge sweep might have triggered some hubris in FDR. In his Second Inaugural Address, Roosevelt issued this summons:

Here is the challenge to our democracy.... I see one-third of the nation ill-housed, ill-clad, and ill-nourished. [16]

Roosevelt's resonant voice did justice to the crafted lines of Sam Rosenman, but it also hinted at social welfare legislation unprecedented in history.

To accomplish that, he needed a Supreme Court not hostile to his objective, but friendly. The solution was to create a different court by adding new members. FDR had overweening confidence that he could remodel the Third Branch of Government to his own fashion. The Court-packing legislation even alarmed some of his own Democrats—not all of them from the South.

For the first time in a decade, Republicans would score gains in Congress. They picked up eighty-one seats in the House and eight in the Senate. FDR's legislative program was the first casualty. Democrats and Republicans who made common cause to stop the Court-packing plan now found it easy to work together to combat other White House initiatives.

But the American newspaper headlines were shifting from politics to foreign policy. Hitler annexed Austria in March 1938. Japan invaded China in 1939. The Spanish Civil War, which had commenced in 1936, would eventually cost the lives of 650,000 combatants. Roosevelt's approach to international issues was intuitive. And idiosyncratic. His one consistency was hatred of war.

In 1936, FDR had delivered a lecture at Chautauqua whose speakers included such luminaries as world traveler Lowell Thomas, author John Gunther, and novelists Pearl Buck and Sinclair Lewis.

Judge Sam Rosenman wrote the draft. But the closing sentences are Churchillian:

> I have seen war. I have seen war on land and sea. I have seen blood running from the wounded. I have seen men coughing out their gassed lungs. I have seen the dead in the mud. . . . I have seen children starving, I have seen the agony of mothers and wives. I hate war.[17]

He ended poetically:

> I can at least make clear that the conscience of America revolts against war and that any Nation which provokes war forfeits the sympathy of people of the United States.[18]

If the 1938 election made FDR appear vulnerable to the politicians, the darkening war clouds in Europe offered a valid rationale to stick with the president.

In August 1940, Roosevelt met Sir Winston Churchill in a secret rendezvous upon the Atlantic Ocean on the battleship HMCS *Prince of Wales*. Churchill, who had been British prime minister since May, begged Roosevelt for a Declaration of War. Roosevelt's answer was that he was skating on thin ice with Congress and they would debate the declaration for three months. Roosevelt advanced for the first time his "Four Freedoms." This was the most enduring result of the meeting: the "Atlantic Charter." While Roosevelt met off Newfoundland with Churchill, Congress wrestled with the bill to extend the draft. It narrowly passed, 203 for and 202 against.

The Republicans in 1940 nominated Wendell Willkie. His huggy-bear looks made him a Republican with sex appeal. Actually, Willkie had been a life-long Democrat. He had supported Wilson's League and backed unlimited aid to Britain. He became a Republican because he distrusted, as a threat to individual liberty, FDR's try for an unprecedented third term, as proof positive of the president's regal ambitions.

FDR picked Secretary of Agriculture Henry Wallace as his running mate to win the farm belt against the corporate lawyer Willkie. Willkie campaigned strenuously, visiting 31 states and delivering 560 speeches. As Willkie's numbers in the polls increased, he became the peace candidate and FDR the warmonger.

FDR then took the offensive:

> I have said it before, but I shall say it again and again and again; your boys are not going to be sent into any foreign wars. [19]

On November 5, 1940, 50 million went to the polls, the largest number ever. FDR, however, won easily with 449 electoral votes to Willkie's 82.

In late 1940, Robert Sherwood, prize-winning playwright of *Abe Lincoln in Illinois*, joined the White House staff at Hopkins' request. At a press conference on December 17, 1940, reporters wanted to challenge the president on his Lend-Lease initiative.

To one journalist's question, the president answered: "Suppose my neighbor's home catches fire and I have a length of garden hose. Would I not lend it to him?"[20] Sherwood had offered this analogy to the president, and FDR hit the question out of the park.

Weeks later, Sherwood came up with another memorable phrase. For a Fireside Chat, he wrote: "We must become the arsenal of democracy."[21]

Actually, Sherwood had borrowed this phrase from Jean Monnet, the Gaullist exile in London. For a Fireside Chat in September 1941, another analogy popped from the imaginative mind of Sherwood:

> When you see a rattlesnake poised to strike, you do not wait until he has struck to crush him. [22]

The president was asking for destroyers to attack the "rattlesnake" U-Boats that were sinking U.S. Merchant Marine ships. Three months later, war made such requests a necessity.

On December 7, 1941, at 1:40 p.m., Roosevelt heard the first reports of Pearl Harbor's bombardment. Alone at the White House on a Sunday, Roosevelt wrote out a brief message to accompany his Declaration of War. As he was drafting his speech, he could hear outside the White House fence crowds singing patriotic songs such as "God Bless America" and "America The Beautiful."

Though he usually depended on speechwriters, his brief but eloquent speech revealed his rarely used talent for English expression. It has to be one of the most famous (as well as most imitated) of his career. Powerfully delivered in his measured and resolute voice, it captured the mood of the American people and Congress

> Yesterday, December 7, 1941—a date which will live in infamy—the United States was suddenly and deliberately attacked by naval and air forces of the Empire of Japan. [23]

After emphasizing the perfidy and treachery of the Japanese, Roosevelt recited a litany of their attacks and the loss of American lives. He closed with this peroration:

> With confidence in our armed forces—with the unbounding determination of our people—we will gain the inevitable triumph—so help us God.[24]

That this was Roosevelt's sole creation is manifest by two words, "infamy" and "unbounding." "Infamy" is a lawyer's word with which FDR was familiar when he helped win a case for his cousin Theodore in 1913. "Unbounding" is a sailor's adjective (instead of the more proper "unbounded"). Both are words never heard before or since in presidential speeches.

Once war was declared against the Axis powers, America quickly mobilized. Supreme Court Justice Jimmy Byrnes was pulled off the bench to become "assistant president for mobilization"—with an office in the White House. Byrnes was preeminently qualified to make things happen. As the consummate Washington insider, he had been a former congressman and senator.

Roosevelt was not so successful in the initial stage of the war. The Germans defeated the American army at Kasserin Pass. Also, FDR alienated the Free French by not recognizing or working with DeGaulle, but FDR later would reluctantly back DeGaulle at Churchill's request. In January 1943, FDR would celebrate his sixty-first birthday in Casablanca at a meeting with Churchill.

As Commander-in-Chief, FDR was a source of inspiration to all the servicemen and women abroad, but as Chief Executive, the alphabet soup of agencies he had created had soured his approval back home. Agencies overlapped and competed with each other. The tangle of multiplying red tape and mountains of paperwork took its toll in the 1942 off-year election. For the first time in the FDR presidency, Roosevelt commanded only a slim (218–208) majority in the House. In the Senate, FDR had to rely on the white supremacist votes in the "Solid South."

But then the war with Germany would turn towards the Allies. In North Africa the war ended in May 1943 when 250,000 Germans and Italians surrendered. The invasion of Sicily could then take place. It was the stepping-stone to Italy and the mainland of Europe.

The Teheran Conference in November 1943—despite Stalin's protests—settled on May 1944 for the invasion of Normandy. (It was later delayed to June.)

In his State of the Union Address on January 11, 1944, FDR combined the perils of tyranny abroad and poverty at home by reasserting the Four Freedoms. The phrases that he himself coined would be subjects of Norman Rockwell's "Saturday Evening Post" covers. Roosevelt had added two freedoms to freedom of speech and freedom of religion: freedom from fear and freedom from want.

> And an equally basic essential to peace is a decent standard of living for all individual men and women and children in all nations. Freedom from fear is eternally linked with freedom from want.[25]

Then FDR specified what he called "a Second Bill of Rights" under which a new basis for security and prosperity could be established regardless of station, race, or creed. Included was a right to a job, a decent home, adequate medical care, and a good education. The Second Bill of Rights was a "cradle to grave" welfare state. It would be the progressive platform of future Democratic National Conventions.

The successful landing of the Allies on D-Day, 1944, should have ensured FDR's victory in November. The new governor of New York, Thomas Dewey, was his Republican opponent. But Dewey was just the visible foe; the invisible foe was death.

Harry Truman replaced Wallace—the darling of the left-wing radicals—to appease the South and the Border moderates. After Truman met the president for the first time to wish him well for his campaign tour of the country, Roosevelt would stay in Washington except for trips to Hawaii and Alaska by ship. They were designed to be restorative of his health.

Truman later said to his nephew, John Truman, who told this writer, "When I looked at him in 1944, I knew I would become president. He was a dying man."

In September 1944, polls told a worried White House that the New York governor was closing the gap. More than any other political foe, Roosevelt loathed his fellow New Yorker, Dewey. He scorned him as "the boy orator of the platitude," a phrase adapted from the description of William Jennings Bryan, "the boy orator of the Platte."

Dewey didn't dare to bring up FDR's frail health, which would only trigger sympathy. So he would allude to the health issue by indirection. He would assert that after twelve years the Administration had become "old and tired," the government was "worn out," the stewardship of policies and programs "weary." The innuendo of declining health by Dewey in his sententious and pompous platitudes riled Roosevelt. Dewey would cap it by a call for "new and vigorous leadership." For FDR to answer the age and health issue directly would only bring attention to it.

The reply would be one of ridicule. An old politico and playwright would pool their talents on one of the best campaign speeches in history. Sam Rosenman and Robert Sherwood would have the president spoof the Republicans in this mock-heroic attack. It would be delivered to the Teamsters'

Union at the Statler-Hilton Hotel on September 23 in Washington and would be an occasion to scotch the health rumors.

Roosevelt began from his place at the podium:

> Well, here we are together again—after four years—and what years they have been! (and he rolled his eyes upward in derision). You know, I am actually four years older, which is a fact that seems to annoy some people. In fact, in the mathematical field there are millions of Americans who are more than eleven years older than when we started in to clear up the mess that was dumped in our laps in 1933.[26]

Then he alluded to some of the progressive-sounding statements of Dewey's.

> Now, imitation may be the sincerest form of flattery—but I am afraid that in this case it is the most common or garden variety of fraud.[27]

Roosevelt continued:

> Of course, it is perfectly true that there are enlightened, liberal elements in the Republican Party. . . . Can the Old Guard pass itself off as the New Deal? I think not. We have all seen many marvelous stunts in the circus but no performing elephant could turn a handspring without falling flat on his back.[28]

The crowd now erupted in uproarious applause. Later in his remarks—in the best political humor ever seen in a presidential campaign—Roosevelt responded to Republican attacks that he had sent a destroyer to retrieve his Scottish Terrier, Fala.

> These Republican leaders have not been content with attacks on me, or my wife, or on my sons.[29]

Then he added, in mock sorrowful tones:

> No, not content with that, they now include my little dog, Fala.[30]

The audience began to roar.

> Well, of course, I don't resent attacks, and my family doesn't resent attacks, but Fala does resent them.[31]

Then with both brows arched high on his forehead:

> You know, Fala is Scotch, and being a Scottie, as soon as he learned that the Republican fiction writers in Congress and out had concocted a story that I had left him behind on the Aleutian Islands and had sent a destroyer back to find

him—at a cost to the taxpayers of two or three, or eight or twenty million dollars—his Scotch soul was furious. He has not been the same dog since.[32]

The volume of laughter in the ballroom rung to the rafters. Roosevelt paused to let the laughter vibrate, and added:

I am accustomed to hearing malicious falsehoods about myself—such as that old, worm-eaten chestnut that I have represented myself as indispensable. But I think I have a right to resent, to object to any libelous statements about my dog.[33]

FDR's return to the campaign trail triggered a resurgence in his popular vote. He would win handily. But a weary president sat for the first time to deliver his Fourth Inaugural Address. It was the second shortest in history. (The briefest was George Washington's in 1793.) Though it only lasted six minutes, it ended:

So we pray to Him now for the vision to see our way clearly, to see the way that leads to a better life for ourselves and for all our fellow men, to the achievement of His will to peace on earth.[34]

Although the address was only six minutes long, Roosevelt told his son, Jimmy, that he had a pain in his heart. Resting briefly in the White House Green Room before proceeding to the receptions, he said, "Jimmy, I can't take this unless you give me a stiff drink."[35]

In April of 1945, the frail and spent president needed a chance to rest and recoup his energies after Yalta had left him in a state of near total exhaustion. Accordingly, the president journeyed by train to Warm Springs. At the arrangement of his daughter, Anna, his long-time intimate friend, Lucy Rutherford, joined him. Their romance had almost broken up his marriage in 1919.

The president had only one item on his agenda during his Warm Springs sojourn: the speech he would read by telephone for the Jefferson–Jackson Day dinner on April 13. Sherwood and Rosenman submitted a draft. Roosevelt would add his own valedictory on a yellow-lined legal sheet as he posed for an informal portrait by Elizabeth Shoumatoff. He summoned from his last reserves this final sentence.

The only limit to our realization of tomorrow will be our doubts of today. Let us move forward with strong and active faith.[36]

These were the words formed by his hand as he slumped with a cerebral stroke. Roosevelt had at his summons a host of wordsmiths, but he always left his imprint on speeches written in his name. To his countrymen in the Depression, he emanated hope, and during the war, unrelenting resolve.

NOTES

1. Humes, *My Fellow Americans*, 153.

2. Ibid., 155.

3. Ibid., 156.

4. Ibid.

5. Walter Lippmann, "The Candidacy of Franklin D. Roosevelt," *The New York Herald Tribune*, January 8, 1932, quoted in James C. Humes, *The Wit & Wisdom of FDR* (New York: Harper Perennial, 2008), 41.

6. Humes, *My Fellow Americans*, 157.

7. Ibid., 158.

8. Ibid.

9. Ibid., 159.

10. Franklin D. Roosevelt, "'More Important Than Gold': FDR's First Fireside Chat" (March 12, 1933), *History Matters: The U.S. Survey Course on the Web*, George Mason University/City University of New York, accessed August 30, 2015, http://historymatters.gmu.edu/d/5199/.

11. Kenneth S. Davis, *FDR: The New Deal Years, 1933–1937* (New York: Random House, 1979), 60.

12. Franklin D. Roosevelt, "Fireside Chat on Banking" (March 12, 1933), John T. Woolley and Gerhard Peters, eds., *The American Presidency Project*, University of California, Santa Barbara, accessed August 28, 2015, http://www.presidency.ucsb.edu/ws/?pid=14540.

13. Franklin D. Roosevelt, "Acceptance Speech for the Renomination for the Presidency, Philadelphia, Pa." (Speech before the 1936 Democratic National Convention, June 27, 1936). John T. Woolley and Gerhard Peters, eds., *The American Presidency Project*, University of California, Santa Barbara, accessed August 5, 2015, http://www.presidency.ucsb.edu/ws/?pid=15314.

14. Davis, *FDR*, 637.

15. Ibid.

16. Franklin D. Roosevelt, "Inaugural Address" (January 20, 1937, Washington, D.C.), John T. Woolley and Gerhard Peters, eds., *The American Presidency Project*, University of California, Santa Barbara, accessed August 2, 2015, http://www.presidency.ucsb.edu/ws/index.php?pid=15349.

17. Franklin D. Roosevelt, "Address at Chautauqua, N.Y. August 14, 1936," John T. Woolley and Gerhard Peters, eds., *The American Presidency Project*, University of California, Santa Barbara, accessed August 3, 2015, http://www.presidency.ucsb.edu/ws/index.php?pid=15097&st=&st1=.

18. Ibid.

19. Franklin D. Roosevelt, "Campaign Address at Boston, Massachusetts" (October 30, 1940), John T. Woolley and Gerhard Peters, eds., *The American Presidency Project*, University of California, Santa Barbara, accessed August 3, 2015, http://www.presidency.ucsb.edu/ws/index.php?pid=15887&st=&st1=.

20. Franklin D. Roosevelt, "Franklin D. Roosevelt Presidential Library and Museum: Our Documents: Lend Lease" (Press Conference of December 17, 1940), *Marist College Archives, Franklin D. Roosevelt Presidential Library and Museum*, accessed August 20, 2014, http://docs.fdrlibrary.marist.edu/odllpc2.html.

21. Franklin D. Roosevelt, "Fireside Chat" (December 29, 1940), John T. Woolley and Gerhard Peters, eds., *The American Presidency Project*, University of California, Santa Barbara, accessed August 20, 2014, http://www.presidency.ucsb.edu/ws/?pid=15917.

22. Franklin D. Roosevelt, "President Franklin Delano Roosevelt Fireside Chat, Rattlesnakes of the Ocean, 9-11-1941," *American Merchant Marine at War, usmm.org*, accessed August 20, 2014, http://www.usmm.org/fdr/rattlesnake.html.

23. Franklin D. Roosevelt, "Pearl Harbor Address to the Nation, December 8, 1941, Washington, D.C.," *American Rhetoric*, accessed August 20, 2014, http://www.americanrhetoric.com/speeches/fdrpearlharbor.htm.

24. Ibid.

25. Franklin D. Roosevelt, "1944 State of the Union Address: FDR's *Second Bill of Rights* or *Economic Bill of Rights* Speech" (January 11, 1944), *Marist College Archives, Franklin D. Roosevelt Presidential Library and Museum,* accessed August 20, 2014, http://www.fdrlibrary.marist.edu/archives/stateoftheunion.html.

26. Franklin D. Roosevelt, "FDR—The Fala Speech" (Campaign dinner address to the International Brotherhood of Teamsters, Chauffeurs, Warehousemen, and Helpers of America, September 23, 1944, Washington, D.C.), *WyzAnt Resources,* accessed August 20, 2014, http://www.wyzant.com/resources/lessons/history/hpol/fdr/fala.

27. Ibid.
28. Ibid.
29. Ibid.
30. Ibid.
31. Ibid.
32. Ibid.
33. Ibid.

34. Franklin D. Roosevelt, "Fourth Inaugural Address. U.S. Inaugural Addresses" (January 20, 1945, Washington, D.C.), *Bartleby.com,* accessed August 20, 2014, http://www.bartleby.com/124/pres52.html.

35. Jean Edward Smith, *FDR* (New York: Random House), 2007, 629.

36. Franklin D. Roosevelt, "Master Speech File, 1898–1945" (Box 3-14, Draft of Jefferson Day Dinner Speech [last undelivered speech], April 13, 1945), *Marist College Archives, Franklin D. Roosevelt Presidential Library and Museum,* accessed August 20, 2014, http://www.fdrlibrary.marist.edu/archives/collections/franklin/index.php?p=collections/findingaid&id=460.

Chapter Twelve

Harry Truman Extends America's Promise

The oldest surviving presidential speechwriter may have been the most instrumental in getting his boss re-elected. Ken Hechler in his century of service to his country wore many hats: Ivy League academic, World War II colonel, and West Virginia congressman.

We both spoke at a conclave honoring descendants of presidents in Marshfield, Missouri in April 2013.

As a former White House speechwriter, I asked him what he did. Ken was modestly dismissive. "I was just a stoker of the fire in 1948—stirring the coals to warm up the president for his 'Give 'em Hell, Harry' talks from the back of the train."[1] "Whistle stop" was the pejorative with which Senator Robert Taft tagged the Democrats' campaign train.[2] "Whistle stop!" answered Truman. "Why, it included Detroit, Denver and L.A."[3]

Anyway, as Ken Hechler told me, he would disembark from the train and check out the gathering crowd until he found a barrel-chested guy in his bib overalls and whisper to him, "When the president comes out to the back of the train, yell, 'Give 'em Hell, Harry,' and Truman would then respond, 'I only tell them the truth and those Republicans think it's hell.' And the president was then all fired up to unleash his staccato attacks."[4]

"At the next stop," said Ken, "I might catch up with a farmer looking like he had been the model of Grant Woods' pitch-forked guy with his wife in that portrait and tell him to shout 'Give those Republicans hell, Harry.'[5] 'No,' Truman would answer, 'I just want them to do their job, to come back to Washington for my Turnip Day Session and put into law all those things for the farmers, the veterans and the workers that they pledged in the pretty platform they wrote.'"[6]

The 1948 campaign seemed mismatched. The polls were making Truman a long shot to beat the smooth-talking Governor Thomas Dewey of New York. Smelling defeat, the Southern Democrats had broken away to start up their own "Dixiecrat Party" and the Northern left wing split off to back former Vice President Henry Wallace in the Progressive Party.

"To hear Truman read a speech was painful," said Hechler, "If FDR spoke like a Commander-in-Chief, Truman sounded like a clerk—a bank clerk, possibly, and he read his talk like a bank statement."[7]

Hechler thought his boss did so much better when he spoke off-the-cuff that Hechler recommended just giving him a list of bullet points and then letting the president wing it from there.

True, Truman's flat Midwestern nasal twang was hardly a match for Dewey's baritone platitudes (Dewey, who boasted a sonorous voice, had once studied for opera). But in the end Truman personified John Q. Public—mad as hell at the way things were going and a lot more believable than the stagey Dewey, who had more style than substance.

Hechler's journey to Truman's side began in the fall of 1947 when he took some of his Princeton students to the White House.[8] The uncle of one of his students was Clark Clifford, the head of Truman's speechwriting staff. Hechler was taken in to meet the president. Truman said to him, "They say I'm causing the welfare state. Can you write me a paper stating how Alexander Hamilton started 'the corporate state'?"[9]

Hechler did, and later he was called by Clark Clifford to come down to Washington and write some speeches. Hechler would assemble these punchy catchy phrases for the president, and in his own conversational style, Truman would pepper the crowds with comments about that "no good, do-nothing Republican Congress."[10]

Like "Old Hickory," "Give 'em Hell" Harry sandbagged the opposition party by setting them up as "the party of privilege" and knocking them down with a strong dose of populist demagoguery.[11]

Old campaigner Truman always maintained he would win, but he was just about the only one who thought so. On Election Night in the White House, Truman would say he heard H.V. Kaltenborn on NBC in his guttural German accent pontificate a Dewey win "when the farm vote comes in."[12]

As Truman told it, "I turned the radio off, had a glass of buttermilk and went to bed."[13]

The farm vote did come in—for Truman! Truman was no longer "the accidental president." Freed from the shadow of Roosevelt, he now basked in the glow of vindication and victory.

Clark Clifford was a fellow Missourian from St. Louis, who first came to Truman's attention as his naval aide. A lawyer by profession, he soon became a trouble-shooter for the president. When Secretary of State George Marshall resigned during the election year in protest of Truman's recognizing Israel, Truman sent the urbane Clifford to talk to Marshall and remind the General of the military chain of command—in other words, that Truman was his superior as Commander-in-Chief. Marshall agreed to keep quiet on his opinions.

In later years, Clifford became an "éminence grise" in Washington's legal world and would be appointed by Lyndon Johnson to succeed McNamara as Secretary of Defense in 1967. But two decades earlier, he had been Truman's "guy-to-go" under Dean Acheson, who succeeded Marshall and advised Truman to devote his Inaugural Address to foreign policy. Truman knew it would be breaking precedent. No other inaugural in history had focused solely on the international situation.

For drafting such an address, which would be read and studied in capitals around the world, Clark Clifford selected someone who would write as a statesman, not as a politician.

George Elsey, a Navy man like Clifford, served as a military advisor to Truman and had traveled with the president to Potsdam in 1945. Only thirty years old, Elsey had as his specialties foreign policy and national security matters. It was his demanding task to have the president defend foreign aid, which had grown increasingly unpopular with Congress and the American people.

Truman was jaunty on Thursday, January 20, 1949. Standing at the podium at 1:30 p.m., Truman put aside his hat, white scarf, and dark overcoat. He stood bareheaded in the wind, his right hand raised as he took his oath of office from his appointee, Chief Justice Fred Vinson, and—as president for the first time in his own right—turned to face the microphones and expectant crowd.

He opened:

> Mr. Vice President, Mr. Chief Justice and Fellow Citizens, I accept with humility the honor which the American people have conferred upon me. I accept it with deep resolve to do all that I can for the welfare of this nation and for the peace of the world. [14]

How strange the matter-of-fact Missouri twang sounded to a world still familiar with a previous president's Harvard phrasing and diction! Truman continued:

> Each period of our national history has had its special challenges. Those that confront us now are as momentous as any in the past. Today marks the beginning not only of a new Administration, but of a period that will be eventful, perhaps decisive, for us and the world. [15]

He looked solemn and determined as he read. Truman's voice was surprisingly strong. There was no hesitation. It was plain that he had worked on it and knew every line. Those close by on the platform could see breath frosting the air. Though a major statement of American aspirations, its focus was on the world, "the peace of the world," "world recovery," "people all over the world." He denounced Communism as a false doctrine dependent on deceit and violence. The line between Communism and democracy was clear.

> Communism is based on the belief that man is so weak and inadequate that he is unable to govern himself, and therefore requires the rule of strong masters. Democracy is based on the conviction that man has the moral and intellectual capacity, as well as the inalienable right, to govern himself with reason and fairness.
>
> Communism subjects the individual to arrest without lawful cause, punishment without trial, and forced labor as the chattel of the state. It decrees what information he shall receive, what art he shall produce, what leaders he shall follow, and what thoughts he shall think. Democracy maintains that government is established for the benefit of the individual, and is charged with the responsibility of protecting the rights of the individual and his freedom in the exercise of his abilities.[16]

Truman then turned from the abstract to nations abroad.

> These differences between Communism and democracy do not concern the United States alone. People everywhere are coming to realize that what is involved is material well-being, human dignity and the right to believe in and worship God.[17]

Truman then asserted:

> I state these differences, not to draw issues of belief as such, but because the actions resulting from the Communist philosophy are a threat to the efforts of free nations to bring about world recovery and lasting peace.[18]

Truman then explained his Marshall Plan:

> Almost a year ago, in company with sixteen free nations of Europe, we launched the greatest cooperative economic program in history.[19]

Triumphantly, he added:

> Our efforts have brought new hope to mankind. We have beaten back despair and defeatism. We have saved a number of countries from losing their liberty. Hundreds of millions of people all over the world now agree with us, that we need not have war—that we can have peace. The initiative is ours.[20]

Truman now came to the theme of his address:

In the coming years, our program for peace and freedom will emphasize four major courses of action. First, we will continue to give unfaltering support to the United Nations. . . . Second, . . . world economic recovery. . . . We believe that our partners in this effort will achieve the status of self-supporting nations once again. [. . .] Third, we will strengthen freedom-loving nations against the dangers of aggression.

We are now working out with a number of countries a joint agreement designed to strenthen the security of the North Atlantic area.[21]

This would be realized as the North Atlantic Treaty Organization (NATO). Truman paused now to introduce Point Four, his bold new kind of aid program:

I believe that we should make available to peace-loving peoples the benefits of our store of technical knowledge in order to help them realize their aspirations for a better life. And, in cooperation with other nations, we should foster capital investment in areas needing development.[22]

Truman explained the purpose of Point Four:

Our aim should be to help the free peoples of the world, through their own efforts, to produce more food, more clothing, more materials for housing, and more mechanical power to lighten their burdens. [. . .] The old imperialism—exploitation for foreign profit—has no place in our plans. Democracy alone can supply the vitalizing force to stir the peoples of the world into triumphant action—not only against their human oppressors, but also against their ancient enemies—hunger, misery, and despair.[23]

Elsey would have Truman close with this repetitive guarantee:

We are aided by all who wish to live in freedom from fear—even by those who live today in fear under their own governments.

We are aided by all who want relief from the lies of propaganda—who desire truth and sincerity.

We are aided by all who desire self-government and a voice in deciding their own affairs.

We are aided by all who long for economic security—for security and abundance that men in free societies can enjoy.

We are aided by all who desire freedom of speech, freedom of religion, and freedom to live their own lives for useful ends.

Our allies are the millions who hunger and thirst after righteousness.[24]

The applause was huge and sustained. Truman was extending the promise of America beyond America. They were the words of a statesman. Many thought it was the finest speech he ever delivered.

The leader of the largest democracy in the world was now the leader of the free world. It was an address that Franklin Roosevelt, Theodore Roosevelt, Woodrow Wilson, and Abraham Lincoln all would have approved and applauded.

NOTES

1. Ken Hechler, interview by James C. Humes, handwritten notes, Marshfield, MO, April 26, 2013.

2. Michael Waldman, *My Fellow Americans: The Most Important Speeches of America's Presidents from George Washington to Barack Obama* (Naperville, IL: Sourcebooks, 2010), 137.

3. Hechler, interview by Humes, April 26, 2013.

4. Humes, *My Fellow Americans,* 177.

5. Hechler, interview by Humes, April 26, 2013.

6. Humes, *My Fellow Americans,* 176.

7. Hechler, interview by Humes, April 26, 2013.

8. Ibid.

9. Ken Hechler, "Truman Library—Ken Hechler Oral History Interview, November 29, 1985" (Interview by Niel M. Johnson), *Harry S Truman Library and Museum Website,* accessed August 16, 2015, https://www.trumanlibrary.org/oralhist/hechler.htm.

10. Hechler, interview by Humes, April 26, 2013.

11. Humes, *My Fellow Americans,* 179.

12. Ibid.

13. Philip White, *Whistlestop: How 31,000 Miles of Train Travel, 352 Speeches, and a Little Midwest Gumption Saved the Presidency of Harry Truman* (Lebanon, NH: ForeEdge [University Press of New England]), 2014, 237.

14. Remini and Golway, *Fellow Citizens,* 361.

15. Ibid.

16. Ibid., 362.

17. Ibid.

18. Ibid.

19. Ibid., 363.

20. Ibid.

21. Ibid., 363–364.

22. Ibid., 365.

23. Ibid.

24. Ibid., 366.

Chapter Thirteen

President Eisenhower's Prophesies

Two of the greatest speeches in American history were delivered in the same week by two U.S. presidents. On Inauguration Day, January 20, 1961, John Kennedy delivered one of the most celebrated and most quoted inaugural addresses. Four days previously, Eisenhower had given his Farewell Address to the American people.

The spectacular pageant of the glamorous and youngest president taking the oath of office has made the public forget the fact that General Eisenhower delivered his valedictory four days earlier.

George Washington was Eisenhower's role model and the president he most esteemed. Like Eisenhower, he was neither a professional politician nor a polished speaker. He was a soldier who answered the call of duty. If Lincoln is credited with saving the Union, it was Washington who actually established that Union. That was why Eisenhower believed that our first president was our greatest.

It was a presidential speechwriter who first planted the idea in Eisenhower's head to emulate Washington and issue a Farewell Address.

Malcolm Moos had come to the White House in Eisenhower's second term. Moos had been a political science professor at Johns Hopkins University in Baltimore, whose president was Eisenhower's younger brother, Milton. A Minnesotan, Moos had written a history of the Republican Party. Dr. Eisenhower had read the history and recommended him to his brother. Moos, whose father had been a Theodore Roosevelt Republican, had a centrist approach to politics, a viewpoint that would appeal to Eisenhower.

Moos, like any speechwriter, had studied the background and philosophy of the president for whom he was writing, and learned that Washington was the soldier–statesman that Eisenhower admired the most.

Eisenhower had just suffered the ordeal of Richard Nixon's razor-edge defeat. If Dick Nixon was not an ideal candidate, he was far preferable to the inexperienced Kennedy. Eisenhower believed Nixon was the most qualified presidential candidate in history.

As for Rockefeller, Eisenhower never forgave the New York governor for his attack on his administration's "missile gap" that didn't exist. During his presidency, Eisenhower was the most popular name in the world. In India in 1959, millions welcomed him with placards proclaiming him "Prince of Peace." Yet the election of 1960 was now being viewed as a referendum on his presidency.

"Do-nothing president!" cried the Democrats. Did "doing nothing" mean getting into no wars and suffering no deaths and casualties for eight years? Did "doing nothing" mean no deficits for six out of eight years? Did the country forget the National Highway program and St. Lawrence Seaway, which helped cause a record U.S. prosperity? Civil rights? Did his critics forget that his was the first administration to enact two civil rights measures as well as his sending troops to Arkansas that broke up Governor Orval Faubus' segregated schools?

But the image of a passive presidency prevailed and the country would pin its hopes on a young and vibrant Senator Kennedy in "getting their country moving again."

Eisenhower had been stung by the newspaper criticism of him as a man bereft of action. After all, Eisenhower had organized the victorious landings of the greatest continental invasion in history. He told Moos of his desire "to have something really significant to say when I leave the White House."[1]

Eisenhower's relationship with speechwriters and staff was cordial but curt. Candidate Ike had a grin as wide as his home state of Kansas, but once he sat down at his desk in the Oval Office, he parked the smile outside. "Eisenhower" in German means "Hewer of Iron" and his stern and disciplined approach to government business reflected his military background. A speechwriter, he felt, was not much higher than a non-commissioned officer when he had dealings with the president.

Eisenhower was aware that many in the academic world of political science thought his military background did not prepare him for the presidency. But Eisenhower had more people under his command than FDR had when he assumed the presidency in 1933. And as supreme commander he was called on to negotiate diplomatic and political arrangements with heads of government and sovereign states. If Eisenhower held professional politicians in minimal esteem, he nevertheless mastered the political arts of tact and persuasion.

Eisenhower is the exception to many leaders; he was influenced neither by insecurities about self nor by an inflated ego. He once told a staffer that General Douglas MacArthur suffered from an "eye problem"—an addiction to the perpendicular pronoun.[2] Eisenhower had no insufficiency of ego, but unlike Generals Patton and Montgomery, he could control it. He had no lack of ambition, either. Anyone who rises to the top in both the military and political spheres would have to possess it.

It is forgotten that Major Eisenhower had once written speeches for General MacArthur in Manila. Eisenhower possessed skills in English expression. In English he scored his highest grades at West Point. The guidebook to World War I battlefields he wrote in 1919 caught the eye of General Pershing. He wrote his World War II best seller, *Crusade in Europe*, without any help from speechwriters. Some compared his muscular uncluttered prose with the much-praised memoirs of President Ulysses S. Grant.

A year before the address, Sir Winston Churchill had visited the president in Gettysburg. The two leaders, whose roots were in the nineteenth century, agreed that the modern technology of the twentieth century was a mixed blessing. It brought the enhancement of material benefits but along with it the erosion of individual dignity and rights as well.

Churchill with his usual prophetic insight was envisioning an Orwellian government that might wield new electronic innovations to invade the home and the privacy of individuals. In the same vein, Eisenhower was lamenting the mega-sizing bigness that was dwarfing the individual: not just in government, but the in the mega-corporation and mega-university.

The phrase "military–industrial complex" had come to Eisenhower's attention. It had been coined by Ralph Williams, a writer in the Navy Department. It referred to the impact of military installations on public schools. Public schools had to seek federal compensation to handle the influx of public school students near military bases. This led Eisenhower to ponder the sociological problems that would result in the burgeoning industrial leviathans spawned by military defense contracts.

On January 16, 1961, as the lights blinked for the introduction of the president of the United States, Eisenhower straightened his tie and coughed into a handkerchief.

> This evening I come to you with a message of leave-taking and farewell, and to share a few final thoughts with you, my countrymen.[3]

Eisenhower's tone was low-key and intimate. His tenor was that of observation, not oration. He proceeded to praise Congress, an institution that every president since has more castigated than commended.

> My own relations with the Congress, which began on a remote and tenuous basis when, long ago, a member of the Senate appointed me to West Point, have since ranged to the intimate during the war and immediate post-war period, and finally to the mutually independent during these past years.[4]

Eisenhower himself had chosen the word "intimate," crossing out "close," and he underlined it in his text. He went on to say:

> In this final relationship, the Congress and the Administration have, on most vital issues, cooperated well, to serve the national good rather than mere partisanship. . . . We now stand ten years past the midpoint of a century that has witnessed four major wars among great nations. Three of those involved our own country.[5]

The Russo-Japanese War of 1905 was the exception on the list that included two World Wars and Korea.

> Despite these holocausts America is today the strongest, the most influential and most productive nation in the world.[6]

Then, Eisenhower struck the theme of his address in words that he had underlined in his text:

> Understandably proud of this pre-eminence, we yet realize that America's leadership and prestige depend, not merely upon our unmatched material progress, riches and material strength, but on HOW we use our power in the interest of world peace and human betterment.[7]

During the war, Eisenhower's views had been closer to those of Roosevelt than Churchill in his assessment of Soviet imperialism and the prospect of post-war cooperation. Yet General Eisenhower, who had felt a genuine warmth towards a fellow general like Marshall Zhukov, had sadly come to realize in full measure the implacability of Soviet intentions regarding the destruction of Western democratic ways.

> We face a hostile ideology—global in scope, atheistic in character, ruthless in purpose, and insidious in method.[8]

The danger it posed was of "infinite duration" in the continuing crisis of the Cold War. There would be many calls to find "a miraculous solution" by spending ever-increasing sums on research and development of new weapons. The word "balance" was the touchstone of Eisenhower's middle-of-the-road philosophy. He urged that every such proposal must be weighed in the light of need to maintain balance . . . between cost and hoped-for advantage.

> Our arms must be mighty, ready for instant action, so that no potential aggressor may be tempted to risk his own destruction.[9]

But in mobilizing the manpower and maintaining the necessary strength to combat a global challenge, Eisenhower feared a monster in the making. He made the point with a biblical allusion:

> Until the latest of our world conflicts, the United States had no armaments industry. American makers of plowshares could, with time and as required, make swords as well. But now we can no longer risk emergency improvisation of national defense; we have been compelled to create a permanent armaments industry of vast proportions.[10]

Then, in ringing phrases, the old General delivered the most quoted words in his career of service to the country. The sentence summed up his deepest feelings and gave voice to his greatest fears:

> This conjunction of an immense military establishment and a large arms industry is new in the American experience. The total influence—economic, political, even spiritual—is felt in every city, every Statehouse, every office of the federal government. We recognize the imperative need for this development. Yet we must not fail to comprehend its grave implications.[11]

Then the General delivered his warning:

> In the councils of government, we must guard against the acquisition of unwarranted influence, whether sought or unsought, by the military–industrial complex.[12]

Eisenhower himself had inserted "whether sought or unsought" to Moos' words in last-minute editing, to soften the effect. Eisenhower did not fear the use of some American version of military fascism. What troubled him was the emergence of a powerful military spending lobby that would be fueled by big business.

Seven junior officers—six naval and one army—would follow the five-star general to the Oval Office. Perhaps their limited experience at a less-than-exalted level made them more compliant to the wishes of Pentagon generals and admirals.

In the summer of 1961, this writer was a sergeant-at-arms at a national Republican meeting in Washington. A Congressman, Bob Ellsworth, had just issued his report on how Lyndon Johnson had slashed military appropriations. Eisenhower, who presided over the group, stabbed his pencil into his writing tablet:

"Congressman, who gave you those statistics?"

"General _____, he's a three star general," was Ellsworth's reply.

"Don't count stars with me, Congressman. I put them there. Generals lie," Eisenhower sternly added. Eisenhower knew from first-hand experience the recurring Pentagon problem of endemic waste and inflated estimates.

Yet Eisenhower's volcanic temper would have erupted if he could have heard the "doves" of later years quote him to support some kind of unilateral disarmament vis-a-vis the Soviet Union. In the world of speechwriters, a "cross quote" is a quotation from a noted conservative to support a liberal cause or vice-versa. The "military–industrial complex" is an egregious example.

Eisenhower wanted a defense second to none. Such a weapons system, however, should be tailored to the needs of the free world, not to the lobby of big defense contractors.

As the last Chief Executive who made an effort to balance the fiscal budget each year, he foresaw the disruptive impact of a mammoth defense-spending outlay. But he also perceived the more subtle danger of a military–industrial complex in a free society.

> The potential for the disastrous rise of misplaced power exists and will persist. We must never let the weight of this combination endanger our liberties or democratic processes. We should take nothing for granted. [13]

Eisenhower, with the capitalization and underlining that he added, showed that he had observed the development of that "iron triangle" consisting of the Pentagon, congressional committee chairmen, and defense industry lobbies whose pressure would smother the unorganized citizens' common sense and sound judgment.

Then, after a pause for taking his breath, Eisenhower issued a second warning which, if it is not so popularly remembered, was equally prophetic. The new age of technology and the rise of the massive corporation in financing the development of such sophisticated instruments and weaponry would serve to stifle the entrepreneurship that forged America's economic greatness.

> Today the solitary inventor, tinkering in his shop, has been overshadowed by task forces of scientists in laboratories and testing fields. [14]

Eisenhower could see the individual's role dwarfed and the purpose of the university distorted by the awarding of massive contracts by big government and by business. A draft of Eisenhower's speech with handwritten editing by his brother Milton contains the following passage:

> The free university has been, historically, the fountainhead of free ideas and scientific discovery. But now, partly because of the huge costs involved, research springs not so much from individuals engaged in random pursuit of knowledge, as from public agencies in grim pursuit of specific, predetermined results. For every old blackboard there are now hundreds of new electronic computers. [15]

Eisenhower had agreed with Churchill's observation: "We need engineers in the world—not a world of engineers."[16]

Eisenhower's brother, Milton, also concurred. He wrote: "Modern man worships at the temple of science, but science tells him only what is possible not what is right."[17] For that reason the retiring president warned that "public policy could be the captive of a scientific technological elite."[18]

The philosopher–general reserved his sternest words for those who would let their children or their children's children shoulder the burden of deficit spending. Here he was warning his Democratic successor of the economic cost of political promises he had made in the course of the recent campaign.

> As we peer into society's future, we—you and I, and our government—must avoid the impulse to live only for today, plundering, for our own ease and convenience, the precious resources of tomorrow.[19]

The last president to send fiscally honest budgets to Congress held conservative economic views that seemed almost quaint to the academic opinion of history, but now he appears to have been a Cassandra whose dire predictions have been fulfilled by trillion dollar deficits.

> We cannot mortgage the material assets of our grandchildren without risking the loss also of their political and spiritual heritage.[20]

Eisenhower followed this admonition with an apology—his failure to achieve mutual disarmament:

> I wish I could say tonight that a lasting peace is in sight. Happily, I can say that war has been avoided.[21]

The old soldier then ended his presidential service as he began, with a prayer that he himself had composed:

> We pray that peoples of all faiths, all races, all nations, may have their great human needs satisfied; that those now denied opportunity shall come to enjoy it to the full; that all who yearn for freedom may experience its spiritual blessings; that those who have freedom will understand, also, its heavy responsibilities; that all who are insensitive to the needs of others will learn charity; that the scourges of poverty, disease and ignorance will be made to disappear from the earth, and that, in the goodness of time, all peoples will come to live together in a peace guaranteed by the binding force of mutual respect and love.[22]

To this final text he penned his own postscript:

Now on Friday noon I have become a private citizen of the United States. I am proud to do so. I thank you and good night. [23]

If the prophet's warning was lost in the succeeding president's poetic ideals and hopes a few days later, the General's biblical commandment to his people not to waste their material treasure and so rob posterity will be more telling and timely as the mounting deficit becomes monstrous.

NOTES

1. Humes, *My Fellow Americans*, 198.
2. James C. Humes, *Eisenhower and Churchill: The Partnership That Saved the World* (Roseville, CA: Forum/Prima Publishing, 2001), 125.
3. Humes, *My Fellow Americans*, 199.
4. Ibid.
5. Ibid., 200.
6. Ibid.
7. Ibid.
8. Ibid.
9. Ibid.
10. Ibid., 201.
11. Ibid.
12. Ibid.
13. Ibid., 202.
14. Ibid.
15. Ibid.
16. Ibid.
17. Ibid.
18. Ibid.
19. Ibid.
20. Ibid., 203.
21. Ibid.
22. Ibid.
23. Ibid.

Chapter Fourteen

John F. Kennedy—Symbol over Substance

John F. Kennedy is the only modern president to be an icon. A naval war hero, he was Hollywood handsome with a glamorous wife. The assassination of this young president of unrealized potential traumatized the nation. Overnight he was mourned as a martyr to the cause of peace and justice.

In the five decades since that tragic day in November, some historians look more dispassionately at his presidency. Some unkind critics suggest that he was all icing without the cake. To put it another way, JFK was more style than substance.

If that is true, Kennedy owes much of his image of grace and eloquence to his main speechwriter, Ted Sorensen. At first glance Sorensen's background was totally opposite to Kennedy's. Kennedy was a Boston Catholic and Sorensen a Nebraskan Unitarian; Kennedy a big-city Democrat and Sorensen a Midwestern Republican; Kennedy a war hero and Sorensen a pacifist.

But a closer study reveals that Sorensen's Republican roots were like those of Nebraska Senator George Norris, a progressive Republican who supported Franklin D. Roosevelt's Tennessee Valley Authority. Both JFK and Sorensen shared a disdain for the religiosity and cant of politicians in public as well as the backslapping camaraderie in Congress.

In a conversation with this author in 1986, Sorensen recalled how his father made him memorize and recite Lincoln's "Gettysburg Address" and Bryan's "Cross of Gold" oration.[1] Around the dinner table were heard recitals of Shakespeare's "Funeral Oration" of Antony or Sir Walter Scott's "Breathes there the man with soul so dead, Who never to himself hath said, 'This is my own, my native land!'"[2]

Sorensen told this author that he had re-read the Gettysburg Address and the Inaugural Address of Woodrow Wilson to find inspiration for JFK's

Inaugural Address.[3] Like his boss, Sorensen was steeped in American history. Although the idea for *Profiles in Courage* was Kennedy's, the writing of the book while Kennedy lay flat in his hospital bed was mostly Sorensen's. Kennedy would, however, offer some revision, and would win the Pulitzer Prize for this history.[4]

In the 1960 campaign, Sorensen provided inspirational vignettes out of history for Kennedy to end his short political remarks with inspiration. At airport appearances, Kennedy would deliver his remarks on the theme "Let's get the country moving again." Then he would close with an uplifting story. A typical ending would be this inspirational vignette about Benjamin Franklin:

> At the Constitutional Convention, George Washington presided on a chair whose back pictured a sun low on the horizon. At the end of the convention, the oldest delegate, Benjamin Franklin, rose and said, "I often looked at that chair and speculated over the long months whether it was a picture of a rising or setting sun. Today I know for the first time it is a rising sun. A new day for America, a new dawn for freedom."[5]

Another closer cited Colonel Davenport, the Connecticut patriot.

> In June 1780, the sun was in eclipse so that even at noon, it looked like midnight. In those days, many thought it was the end of the world. In the Connecticut House of Delegates, there was panic and pandemonium. Colonel Davenport, the Speaker of the House, gaveled the chamber into silence. "Gentlemen, the world is either coming to an end or it is not coming to an end. If it is not coming to an end, there is no need to adjourn. If it is coming to an end, I want the Lord finding me doing my duty. I, therefore, will entertain the motion that candles may be brought in so that we can enlighten this hall of democracy."[6]

Kennedy delivered these closers so frequently that Sorensen would indicate the one by a sun low on the horizon and the other by a candle.

Sorensen also told this writer that many of his talks also closed with a biblical quotation. Sorensen had amassed for Kennedy many Old Testament ones—so as not to offend Jewish voters—from a Jewish institute.[7] These biblical references struck a religious chord.

As Kennedy was sworn in on his family Bible (Doury) by Chief Justice Warren, the new chief executive looked nothing like the scrawnier twenty-nine year old who had taken his congressional oath fourteen years before. The maturing years, not to mention his daily shots for Addison's disease, had filled out his face, and television seemed to add weight to an appearance that up close seemed less forceful.

Kennedy certainly offered the most handsome presence since Harding and his vibrancy and style suggested the most lively presidency since Theodore Roosevelt's.

He opened loftily in lines that owed much to Wilson's First Inaugural. The voice was high and the accent a medley of Boston Brahmin and Irish, which muted the "r" of American English.

> We observe today not a victory of party but a celebration of freedom. [8]

Like other presidents before him, he spoke of the constitutional requirement of oaths. He used that reference to invoke our revolutionary beginnings and his generation's response to that heritage.

> We dare not forget today that we are the heirs of that first revolution. Let the word go forth from this time and place, to friend and foe alike, that the torch has been passed to a new generation of Americans—born in this century, tempered by war, disciplined by a hard and bitter peace, proud of our ancient heritage—and unwilling to witness or permit the slow undoing of those human rights to which this Nation has always been committed, and to which we are committed today at home and around the world. [9]

The biblical subjunctive reflected Kennedy's primary direction to Sorensen to write that the post-war generation had now come of age. Then Sorensen had Kennedy deliver a dithyramb reminiscent of Churchill's wartime eloquence, a call to arms. If taken literally it explains and predicts his administration's involvement in Vietnam a year and a half later. Neither Truman nor Eisenhower nor Johnson nor Nixon ever suggested interventionism on such a large scale. The internal rhyme and alliterative phrase were more poetic than practical.

> Let every nation know, whether it wishes us well or ill, that we shall pay any price, bear any burden, meet any hardship, support any friend, oppose any foe, in order to assure the survival and the success of liberty. This much we pledge—and more. [10]

If Kennedy countenanced military intervention, he now coupled it with diplomatic initiatives. In three successive paragraphs he advanced the concept of the Peace Corps in the Third World, the Alliance for Progress in Latin America, and a new reliance on the United Nations.

> To those peoples in the huts and villages across the globe struggling to break the bonds of mass misery, we pledge our best efforts to help them help themselves . . . not because we seek their votes, but because it is right. If a free society cannot help the many who are poor, it cannot save the few who are rich. [11]

Although Kennedy did not mention by name what would later be called the Peace Corps, he hit upon its idealistic appeal with an aphorism that had the beauty of a biblical beatitude. In the second foreign policy commitment, he offered his own update of the Monroe Doctrine as had both Theodore Roosevelt in 1904 and FDR in 1936, with the Good Neighbor Doctrine.

> To our sister republics south of the border, we offer a special pledge—to convert our good words into good deeds—in a new alliance for progress. . . . Let all our neighbors know that we shall join with them to oppose aggression or subversion anywhere in the Americas. [12]

For his third commitment, Kennedy applied Lincoln's phrase about the meaning of democracy.

> To that world assembly of sovereign states, the United Nations, our last best hope in an age where the instruments of war have outpaced the instruments of peace, we renew our pledge of support. [13]

The next line is the only change or addition Kennedy made to the Sorensen draft. He softened Sorensen's "enemy" to "adversary."

> Finally, to those nations who would make themselves our adversary, we offer not a pledge but a request: that both sides begin anew the quest for peace. [14]

From the arms race, Sorensen had Kennedy move to the arms talks with the Soviets, coining this catchy parallelism. This is perhaps the second most quoted inaugural line:

> So let us begin anew—remembering on both sides that civility is not a sign of weakness, and sincerity is always subject to proof. Let us never negotiate out of fear. But let us never fear to negotiate. [15]

Sorensen's musical ear had Kennedy follow a lyrical aphorism with a feminine internal rhyme:

> Let both sides explore what problems unite us instead of belaboring those problems which divide us. [16]

As they did so often in campaign remarks, Unitarian Sorensen and Catholic Kennedy then invoked the moral authority of the Old Testament.

> Let both sides unite to heed in all corners of the earth the command of Isaiah— to "undo the heavy burdens . . . and to let the oppressed go free." [17]

Then, aware of the high expectation of inaugural rhetoric, Sorensen borrowed from Churchill's line, "This is not the end, nay, not even the beginning of the end."[18]

> All this will not be finished in the first one hundred days. Nor will it be finished in the first one thousand days, nor in the life of the Administration, nor even perhaps in our lifetime on this planet. But let us begin.[19]

The speech then refers to the generational theme.

> Since this country was founded, each generation of Americans has been summoned to give testimony to its national loyalty. The graves of young Americans who answered the call to service surround the globe. Now the trumpet summons us again—not a call to bear arms, though arms we need; not as a call to battle, though embattled we are—but a call to bear the burden of a long twilight struggle . . . against the common enemies of man: tyranny, poverty, disease, and war itself.[20]

Like a young King Henry at Agincourt, Kennedy echoes Shakespeare in his summons to his contemporaries to mount the challenge of the Cold War.

> In the long history of the world, only a few generations have been granted the role of defending freedom in its hour of maximum danger. I do not shrink from this responsibility—I welcome it. I do not believe that any of us would exchange places with any other people or any other generation.[21]

Then Kennedy, stabbing his fingers in the air as his nasal twang pierced the heavy January cold, laid the prefatory groundwork like a Greek rhetorician to call attention to the climactic peroration:

> And so my fellow Americans:[22]

Kennedy paused to build audience anticipation.

> Ask not what your country can do for you—ask what you can do for your country.[23]

An electrified audience clapped their numb hands for warmth. No other presidential line had quite so kindled American idealism. Three long minutes later, a dimming applause was ignited by its twin refrain:

> My fellow citizens of the world: ask not what America will do for you, but what together we can do for the freedom of man.[24]

To close, Sorensen gave Kennedy a Churchillian valedictory:

With a good conscience our only sure reward, with history the final judge of
our deeds, let us go forth to lead the land we love, asking His blessing and His
help, but knowing that here on earth God's work must truly be our own.[25]

The hordes of Democrats and Kennedy partisans who braved the January
winds to participate in what they thought would be a milestone event in
American history were not disappointed. Kennedy not only rose to the occasion but transcended it in eloquence that only yields to the sublimity of
Lincoln's Second Inaugural. It was television, however, that transformed a
constitutional creed for the nation's young. Kennedy had directed his remarks to his contemporaries of returning veterans, but the message would
leave its mark on that generation's crop of children: the volunteers for the
Peace Corps, the demonstrators for civil rights, and later the student militants
against Vietnam.

This writer, who was a Pennsylvania legislator at the time of the assassination, was asked to deliver the eulogy.

Into the smoked-filled room, Kennedy brought the sunshine of campus ideals.
By his eloquence and style, politics became public service.[26]

Yet, in a sense, Kennedy's inaugural was the acme of his administration.
The lyric expression of our ideals and hopes were the sole criterion of presidential greatness. JFK would be a candidate for Mount Rushmore. One ad-
mittedly biased observer was the outgoing vice president and Kennedy's
leading opponent, who sat on the platform. Nixon said this to me and others,
"Great poetry—bad policy—the most hawkish speech given by a Cold War
president—and to think the man who drafted it was a pacifist and one-time
conscientious objector."[27]

Some on the left would later say that JFK's rhetoric wasn't matched by
his record. Civil rights activists would credit LBJ, not JFK, for their legislative success, and social welfare leftists would laud Johnson's War on Poverty.

Revisionist biographers may cite CIA plots against the lives of Castro in
Cuba or Diem in Vietnam, the wire-tapping of Dr. Martin Luther King, or
even Kennedy's tawdry liaisons with Marilyn Monroe or Mafiosa mole Ju-
dith Exner. Yet they can never dim the symbolic appeal of hope that his
inaugural presence and eloquence inspired on Inauguration Day. At a time
when politics became theater, Kennedy was its first star.

NOTES

1. Ted Sorensen, conversation with James C. Humes, the Brook Club, New York, NY,
March 1990.
    2. Ibid.

3. Ibid.

4. Humes, *My Fellow Americans,* 211.

5. Ibid., 214.

6. Ibid.

7. Ibid., Notes to Chapter 14, Note 3, 224.

8. Ibid, 219.

9. Ibid.

10. Ibid.

11. Remini and Golway, *Fellow Citizens,* 386.

12. Ibid.

13. Ibid., 387.

14. Ibid.

15. Ibid.

16. Ibid.

17. Ibid.

18. Winston Churchill, "The Bright Gleam of Victory" (A Speech at the Lord Mayor's Day Luncheon at the Mansion House, London, November, 10, 1942), *The Churchill Centre,* accessed September 9, 2015, http://www.winstonchurchill.org/resources/speeches/1941-1945-war-leader/the-end-of-the-beginning.

19. Remini and Golway, *Fellow Citizens,* 388.

20. Ibid.

21. Ibid.

22. Ibid.

23. Ibid.

24. Ibid.

25. Ibid.

26. James C. Humes, Eulogy for President Kennedy delivered to the Pennsylvania Legislature, December 3, 1963.

27. Richard M. Nixon, conversation with James C. Humes and other staffers while packing up Vice President Nixon's papers, January 20, 1961.

Chapter Fifteen

President Lyndon Johnson Declares His Dream for a Great Society

The White House speechwriter who drafted the "Great Society Speech" that President Johnson delivered in Michigan in 1964 was also the originator of the phrase "Great Society."

Johnson, Dick Goodwin said later, was looking for some kind of slogan that might focus on his domestic aims. Goodwin had written for LBJ, "For in your time we have the opportunity to move not only toward the rich society and the powerful society, but upward to the Great Society," and the phrase stuck.[1] When the press began to pick it up, the President liked it, recalled Goodwin. It was decided to follow up with a full-dress speech at Ann Arbor, Michigan.

Johnson was not a "Great Communicator" like Reagan. He was never successful in delivering an address from the Oval Office. Yet he was probably the most gifted one-on-one persuader in White House history. It was an art that had to be watched. Probably the tallest Chief Executive since Lincoln, when Johnson leaned down to engage his listeners, he more than dominated them with his huge presence. But that enfolding mass did not translate across the screen. On television Johnson seemed like he was a journeyman actor trying to play a contemporary President Charles de Gaulle.

Unlike his predecessor John F. Kennedy, he never came close to mastering a televised address. Neither did his Southwestern drawl compare favorably with JFK's Harvard accented words.

At Ann Arbor, Johnson opined:

I have come today from the turmoil of your Capital to the tranquility of your campus to speak about the future of your country.[2]

Johnson was not a gifted speaker like his predecessor, but the written alliteration tried to impart a lyric lift to his cadence.

> The purpose of protecting the life of our Nation and preserving the liberty of our citizens is to pursue the happiness of our people. Our success in that pursuit is the test of our success as a Nation.
> For a century we labored to settle and subdue a continent. [3]

Then Goodwin inserted the adjective "unbounded" to add an echo of FDR.

> For half a century we called upon unbounded invention and untiring industry to create an order of plenty for all our people. [4]

Dick Goodwin knew that LBJ's hero was the New Deal president.

> The challenge of the next half century is whether we have the wisdom to use that wealth to enrich and elevate our national life, and to advance the quality of our American civilization. [5]

With an alliterative touch, Goodwin introduced the phrase, "Great Society."

> Your imagination, your initiative, and your indignation will determine whether we build a society whose progress is the servant of our needs, or a society where old values and new visions are buried under unbridled growth. For in your time we have the opportunity to move not only toward the rich society and the powerful society, but upward to the Great Society. [6]

Now President Johnson would define his Great Society:

> The Great Society is a place where every child can find knowledge to enrich his mind and to enlarge his talents. It is a place where leisure is a welcome chance to build and reflect, not a feared cause of boredom and restlessness. It is a place where the city of man serves not only the needs of the body and the demands of commerce, but the desire for beauty and the hunger for community. [7]

The old Baptist and one-time high school teacher Johnson now turns from the material to the spiritual, when he defines the Great Society using both alliteration and rhyme.

> It is a place where man enhances his contact with nature. It is a place which honors creation for its own sake for what it adds to the understanding of the race. It is a place where men are more concerned with the quality of their goals than the quantity of their goods. [8]

If the Johnson drawl was not friendly to the resonance of alliteration or the rhetoric of rhyme, it approached eloquence.

> But most of all, the Great Society is not a safe harbor, a resting place, a final objective, a finished work. It is a challenge constantly renewed, beckoning us toward a destiny where the meaning of our lives imitates the marvelous products of our labor. [9]

If with those words Johnson employed the past advice of Goodwin, they had not the JFK appeal. The Johnson Southwestern drawl lacked the vigor and vibrancy of the martyred president's Boston accent.

Johnson now listed the places to build the Great Society—in the cities, in our countryside, and in our classrooms.

> Aristotle said, "Men come together in cities in order to live, but they remain together in order to live the good life." [. . .] Our society will never be great until our cities are great. Today the frontier of our imagination and innovation is inside those cities and not beyond their borders. [. . .]
>
> A second place where we begin to build the Great Society is in our countryside. We have always prided ourselves on being not only America the strong and America the free, but America the beautiful. [10]

LBJ expanded on that theme.

> Today that beauty is in danger. The water we drink, the food we eat, the very air we breathe, are threatened with pollution. Our parks are overcrowded, our seashores overburdened. Green fields and dense forests are disappearing. [11]

The president now cited the novel by Graham Greene.

> A few years ago we were greatly concerned about the "Ugly American." Today we must prevent an ugly America. [12]

The Greene novel reference elicited great applause. Johnson continued:

> For once the battle is lost, once our national splendor is destroyed, it can never be recaptured. And once man can no longer walk with beauty or wonder at nature his spirit will wither and his sustenance be wasted. [13]

The former high school teacher in Texas now turned to the third feature of the Great Society:

> A third place to build the Great Society is in the classrooms of America. There your children's lives will be shaped. Our society will not be great until every young mind is set free to scan the farthest reaches of thought and imagination. [14]

In a ringing aphorism that was applauded, LBJ states,

> Poverty must not be a bar to learning, and learning must offer an escape from poverty. [15]

The president continues with the promise:

> We are going to assemble the best thought and the broadest knowledge from all over the world to find those answers for America. [. . .]
> The solution to these problems does not rest in a massive program in Washington, nor can it rely solely on the strained resources of local authority. They require us to create new concepts of cooperation, a creative federalism, between the National Capital and the leaders of local communities. [16]

Amid the alliterative profusion of "c's," Goodwin offers a new name for his democratic philosophy, "Creative Federalism." Goodwin now has the president cite the first true liberal Democrat of the twentieth century:

> Woodrow Wilson once wrote, "Every man sent out from his university should be a man of his Nation as well as a man of his time." [17]

Johnson ended his peroration with a rhetorical challenge to his audience:

> So, will you join in the battle to give every citizen the full equality which God enjoins and the law requires, whatever his belief, or race, or the color of his skin? Will you join in the battle to give every citizen an escape from the crushing weight of poverty? Will you join in the battle to make it possible for all nations to live in enduring peace—as neighbors and not as mortal enemies? [18]

Johnson closes:

> Those who came to this land sought to build more than just a new country. They sought a new world. So I have come here today to your campus to say that you can make their vision our reality. So let us from this moment begin our work so that in the future men will look back and say: "It was then, after a long and weary way, that man turned the exploits of his genius to the full enrichment of his life." [19]

The address, as it reads, is the equal of anything that JFK ever delivered. But the LBJ style often made the inspirational on paper become the insipid when heard.

Actually, to be objective, Lincoln in his delivery did not inspire or lift his audience at Gettysburg. It read better in print. JFK's biographers do much to liken him to the assassinated Lincoln. But the way Americans looked at

Lincoln before his assassination was much the way of Easterners who were the literary voice of America before the Ford Theater tragedy.

Lincoln was a crude and uneducated rube—a rough Westerner who delighted in regaling his audiences with earthy and bawdy stories. The sublime eloquence of Lincoln at Gettysburg or the Second Inaugural was not yet known.

In Kentucky in 1972, I heard a lawyer named Johnson who claimed to be a fourth cousin of Abraham Lincoln deliver a speech. He was six foot three, the image of his claimed cousin. In fact he was the model for some memorials made of the president. A staunch Republican, he admitted to some kinship to Lyndon Johnson, "But I don't boast of it."

NOTES

1. Richard N. Goodwin, *Remembering America: A Voice from the Sixties* (New York: Harper and Row, 1988), 277.

2. Lyndon B. Johnson, "The Great Society" (Commencement Address to the University of Michigan, Ann Arbor, Michigan, May 22, 1964), *LBJ Library and Museum, The University of Texas,* accessed August 21, 2014, http://www.lbjlib.utexas.edu/johnson/lbjforkids/gsociety_read.shtm.

3. Ibid.
4. Ibid.
5. Ibid.
6. Ibid.
7. Ibid.
8. Ibid.
9. Ibid.
10. Ibid.
11. Ibid.
12. Ibid.
13. Ibid.
14. Ibid.
15. Ibid.
16. Ibid.
17. Ibid.
18. Ibid.
19. Ibid.

Chapter Sixteen

Richard Nixon Mobilizes the Silent Majority

Richard Nixon is the "bête noir" of the Left. The surprising fact is that Nixon accomplished as president many of the promises of the Democratic Party platform that Democrats John Kennedy and Lyndon Johnson could not. They include Affirmative Action, the establishment of the Environmental Protection Agency, ending of the draft, the amendment granting eighteen-year-olds the vote, and the right to vote in the District of Columbia. The first two measures, the unions blocked; the last, Democratic Southern senators would oppose. Then President Nixon, in February 1972, achieved a diplomatic breakthrough in the form of a rapprochement with China—something former British Prime Minister Harold Macmillan called "the diplomatic feat of the century."[1]

Democratic presidents had been politically afraid to attempt such a move whereas the known anti-Communist Nixon could. Yet candidate Nixon had hinted at such a China initiative in *Foreign Affairs* magazine in 1967, two years before he took office.

But it was Nixon's anti-Communist reputation that was at the root of the rancor the intellectual left held against the Californian. Nixon has successfully exposed Alger Hiss, the State Department advisor to FDR at Yalta, as a Communist Party member. The Ivy League Hiss had been a darling of the Democratic left.

Yet although *The New York Times* had praised Nixon's role as fair, the left still smeared Nixon with "McCarthyism." The irony was that Nixon despised Joe McCarthy who, by his excesses, undermined the anti-Communist cause.

It was the Kennedy family who supported McCarthy's campaign with donations. Joe McCarthy had arranged for Robert Kennedy to be put on the

Senate Government Operations Committee as investigative counsel, and Bobby would name him the godfather to his eldest child, Kathleen. It was no coincidence that Senator John F. Kennedy did not vote on the censure of the Wisconsin senator. (Kennedy was in the hospital for his back, but he neglected to send in a proxy or pair with another absent senator.)

Yet it was McCarthyism that rubbed off on the Republican Nixon, not the popular Kennedy. Nixon was not a likable personality as was the glamorous Kennedy. In addition, President Eisenhower had delegated to his young vice president the job of deputy head of party as well as deputy chief of state. In the latter role he would visit 93 countries representing the United States. The other job as chief attacker of Democrats was a two-edged sword. It gave him the nationwide contacts to get the nomination, but it also gave him the partisan image that could defeat his presidential candidacy, for the Republicans were the minority party. After the landslide re-election of Eisenhower and Nixon in 1956, the Californian begged Eisenhower to relieve him of being the Republican hatchet man, but Eisenhower, who liked his above-politics image, refused.

In 1967, while candidates George Romney and Nelson Rockefeller campaigned for the 1968 nomination, Nixon took a trip abroad to Europe and Asia, bringing along his principal speechwriter, Ray Price. Price had been a writer for *The New York Herald Tribune* who drafted their 1964 editorial endorsing Johnson over Goldwater. The Yale graduate would develop almost a father-son relationship with Nixon. In some ways, they were similar—introverts in an extrovert's profession. Well-read in English history, Price admired Nixon's intellectual erudition, and in long talks with Nixon, discovered his fascination with leaders in history.

Nixon would introduce a new kind of technique for campaigning. In his "Man In The Arena" events, Nixon would host focus groups where he would take questions from citizens. His brilliance in answering questions without notes in front of him showed how prepared the world-traveler Nixon was.

A Nixon speechwriter had compiled for the candidate notebooks of quotations from Churchill, De Gaulle, Adenauer, and others who had met Nixon. In his remarks, Nixon would say, "I remember in New Delhi, Dr. Nehru and one of his favorite sayings, 'What the world needs is a generation of peace.'"[2] By such a quotation, Nixon would imply his foreign policy experience. He did not have to specify it in detail.

In long talks with Price, Nixon would discuss his conversations with many world leaders. Churchill in 1954 told Nixon to stay out of Vietnam. His advice was to "send armaments not armies." President De Gaulle had introduced to Nixon a new concept to work toward, "détente" (relaxation of tensions between the feuding Cold War powers). He could do that in Asia by working with Chou En Lai—the ablest Asian diplomat, said the French leader.

With Price, Nixon wrote an article, "Asia After Viet Nam" (*Foreign Affairs,* October 1967), which hinted at a Nixon rapprochement with the People's Republic of China.[3] Nixon, who hated small talk, enjoyed cerebral discussions on policy. On several occasions, Nixon told this writer that sometimes he wished he had pursued an academic instead of a legal career.

Nixon had sensed by the fall of 1968 that the venom and vitriol spewed by the Left against President Johnson the previous year ("Hey, Hey, LBJ, how many men did you kill today?") would soon be directed at him. As president in 1969, Nixon knew he had to lance the boil of dissent before its toxin infected the nation. His strategy was first to have veteran wordsmith Bill Safire write for Vice President Spiro Agnew a searing attack on the bias of the mainstream media. Then he would draft with the more philosophical Price a well-reasoned case for his Vietnam Policy.

For the address televised on November 3, 1969, Nixon would write and re-write a total of fourteen drafts, each of which was re-drafted, edited, and re-edited by Ray Price. That evening, in his resonant baritone, Nixon began in measured tones:

> Good evening, my fellow Americans. Tonight I want to talk to you on a subject of deep concern to all Americans and to many people in all parts of the world—the war in Vietnam. I believe that one of the reasons for the deep division about Vietnam is that many people have lost confidence in what their Government has told them about our policy.[4]

Here Nixon assumes an almost professorial role in his lecture on Vietnam.

> Tonight, therefore, I would like to answer some of the questions that I know are on the minds of many of you listening to me.[5]

Nixon then poses five rhetorical questions:

> How and why did America get involved in Vietnam in the first place?
> How has this administration changed the policy of the previous administration?
> What has really happened in the negotiations in Paris and on the battlefront in Vietnam?
> What choices do we have if we are to end this war?
> What are the prospects for peace?[6]

To answer these questions, Nixon then explains what he found when he took office:

> The war had been going on for four years.
> 31,000 Americans had been killed in action.
> The training program for the South Vietnamese was behind schedule.

540,000 Americans were in Vietnam with no plans to reduce the number.
No progress had been made at the negotiations in Paris and the United States
had not put forth a comprehensive peace proposal.
The war was causing deep division at home and criticism from many of our
friends as well as our enemies abroad. [7]

Nixon had been matter-of-fact in outlining the current situation. He did
not want a hint of partisanship to be allowed to color the options that he
faced.

In view of these circumstances there were some who urged that I end the war
at once by ordering the immediate withdrawal of all American forces. From a
political standpoint this would have been a popular and easy course to follow.
After all, we became involved in the war while my predecessor was in office. I
could blame the defeat which would be the result of my action on him and
come out the Peacemaker. Some put it to me quite bluntly: This was the only
way to avoid allowing Johnson's War to become Nixon's War. [8]

This was a familiar Nixon technique: to pose the easy way and then the
hard and right way.

But I had a greater obligation than to think only of the years of my administration and of the next election. I had to think of the effect of my decision on
the next generation and on the future of peace and freedom in America and in
the world. [. . .]
The question at issue is not whether Johnson's War becomes Nixon's War.
The great question is: How can we win America's peace? [9]

Again, President Nixon assumes the objective professor's role to explain
how America got involved in Vietnam in the first place.

Fifteen years ago, North Vietnam, with the logistical support of Communist
China and the Soviet Union, launched a campaign to impose a Communist
government on South Vietnam by instigating and supporting a revolution.
In response to a request by the Government of South Vietnam, President
Eisenhower sent economic aid and military equipment to prevent a Communist
takeover. Seven years ago, President Kennedy sent 16,000 military personnel
to Vietnam as combat advisers. Four years ago, President Johnson sent
American combat forces to South Vietnam. [10]

Then the president poses the question:

Now that we are in the war, what is the best way to end it? [11]

Nixon then discusses immediate withdrawal, but notes that when troops were removed from North Vietnam the Communists murdered 50,000 people and sent hundreds of thousands more to slave-labor camps.

> For the United States, this first defeat in our Nation's history would result in a collapse of confidence in American leadership, not only in Asia but throughout the world. [12]

Nixon then quotes the martyred John Kennedy.

> In 1963, President Kennedy, with his characteristic eloquence and clarity, said, " . . . we want to see a stable government there, carrying on a struggle to maintain its national independence." [13]

Nixon then cites President Eisenhower and President Johnson as having expressed Kennedy's same commitment to South Vietnam. He then rejects others' counsel to end the war by withdrawing our forces, and announces:

> In order to end a war fought on many fronts, I initiated a pursuit for peace on many fronts. [14]

Nixon explains that these initiatives included the complete withdrawal of all outside forces within a year; a ceasefire under international supervision; and free elections under international supervision. He then refers to North Vietnam's answer: the unconditional withdrawal of U.S. troops, who must overthrow the government of South Vietnam as they leave. Nixon explains to his audience that he tried getting his message directly to Ho Chi Minh by an intermediary who was a friend of the North Vietnamese president. The answer, said Nixon, came three days before the leader's death on August 10: another negative response.

Nixon then outlined again his Guam Doctrine, enunciated the previous July:

> We shall look to the nation directly threatened to assume the primary responsibility of providing the manpower for its defense. [15]

This is what Nixon meant in the pledge made during his campaign to end America's involvement in Vietnam. Price now had Nixon state the policy in blunt Nixonian language.

> In the previous administration, we Americanized the war in Vietnam. In this administration, we are Vietnamizing the search for peace. [16]

Nixon then reviewed his progress to limit American involvement.

After 5 years of Americans going into Vietnam, we are finally bringing American men home. [. . .] The South Vietnamese have continued to gain in strength. [. . .] Enemy infiltration . . . over the last 3 months is less than 20 percent of what it was over the same period last year. [. . .] U.S. casualties have declined. [17]

Nixon summarized his position:

My fellow Americans, I am sure you can recognize from what I have said that we really only have two choices open to us if we want to end this war.

I can order an immediate precipitate withdrawal of all Americans from Vietnam without regard to the effects of that action.

Or we can persist in our search for a just peace through a negotiated settlement if possible, or through continued implementation of our plans for Vietnamization . . . as the South Vietnamese become strong enough to defend their own freedom.

I have chosen this second course.

It is not the easy way.

It is the right way. [18]

Next, Nixon described the war protests he had witnessed.

In San Francisco a few weeks ago, I saw demonstrators carrying signs reading, "Lose in Vietnam, bring the boys home." [19]

Now Nixon answers those critics:

Well, one of the strengths of our free society is that any American has a right to reach that conclusion and to advocate that point of view. But as President of the United States, I would be untrue to my oath of office if I allowed the policy of this Nation to be dictated by the minority who hold that point of view and who try to impose it on the Nation by mounting demonstrations in the street. [20]

The president then turned his attention to the young people who on night-ly television were the in-your-face-demonstrators and protesters against the war.

And now I would like to address a word, if I may, to the young people of this Nation who are particularly concerned, and I understand why they are con-cerned, about this war.

I respect your idealism.

I share your concern for peace.

I want peace as much as you do.

Let historians not record that when America was the most powerful nation in the world we passed on the other side of the road and allowed the last hopes for peace and freedom of millions of people to be suffocated by the forces of totalitarianism. [21]

The president now voiced the phrase that would give its name to his address:

> And so tonight—to you, the great silent majority of my fellow Americans—I ask for your support.[22]

The address was the most successful of his presidency. In a deliberate and measured beat, keeping his eyes on the television audience, he never looked down at his text.

The White House press corps had expected Nixon to withdraw from Vietnam. Nixon's message was that America would stay there until the South Vietnamese were able to defend themselves or until the North Vietnamese negotiated an honorable peace settlement.

In light of this, the Washington press corps abandoned all pretense of making impartial summaries of the speech, as was the usual custom following a nationwide presidential address. Instead they launched their own adversarial attack. This was shown to be a mistake when it became apparent that the Nixon address had found accord with a vocal majority. A Gallop Poll taken right after the talk recorded a 77-percent approval rating. Positive letters to Congress and the White House poured in at unprecedented levels. Nixon's approval rating had sidelined the anti-war movement to a noisy but impotent minority.

As the year ended, Nixon remained elated by the impact of the November 3 telecast. He believed it had brought him enough time to advance both Vietnamization and the Vietnam peace process significantly forward.

NOTES

1. James C. Humes and Jarvis D. Ryals, *"Only Nixon": His Trip to China Revisited and Restudied* (Lanham, Maryland: University Press of America, 2009), 49.

2. James C. Humes, *Confessions of a White House Ghost: Five Presidents and Other Political Adventures* (Washington, D.C.: Regnery, 1997), 119.

3. Richard M. Nixon, "Asia After Viet Nam," *Foreign Affairs,* Vol. 46, No. 1, 111–125, October 1967.

4. Richard M. Nixon, "Address to the Nation on the War in Vietnam" (November 3, 1969), John T. Woolley and Gerhard Peters, eds., *The American Presidency Project, University of California, Santa Barbara,* accessed August 22, 2014, http://www.presidency.ucsb.edu/ws/?pid=2303.

5. Ibid.

6. Ibid.

7. Ibid.

8. Ibid.

9. Ibid.

10. Ibid.

11. Ibid.

12. Ibid.

13. Ibid.

14. Ibid.

15. Ibid.

16. Ibid.
17. Ibid.
18. Ibid.
19. Ibid.
20. Ibid.
21. Ibid.
22. Ibid.

Chapter Seventeen

Gerald Ford Shares Healing Words

If the White House press corps liked Gerry Ford, they also underestimated his intelligence. But then they are overwhelmingly liberal or Democrat—Republican presidents like Ford are not considered mentally quick or bright, except for Nixon, whom they thought "wicked." They were also disparaging about the military man, Eisenhower, and the actor, Reagan. About Ford, they loved to quote LBJ's gibe, "he couldn't walk and chew gum at the same time." They never point out that Ford graduated from Yale Law School with grades higher than his classmate, Cyrus Vance, Carter's former Secretary of State, who confirmed that for me at a lunch in New York.

Ford might not have had the intellectual curiosity of a John Kennedy, but unlike Kennedy, he knew chapter and verse of all important legislation. He could recall in detail items in past military appropriation bills. He was a "legislator's legislator."

But the Washington press continued to paint the Michigan president as an awkward, bumbling fellow, particularly after he slipped and fell down on icy airline stairs one time. The fact is that Gerald Ford, the All-American guard at Michigan and drafted NFL choice of the Detroit Lions, was probably the best natural athlete ever to occupy the White House. But of course that does not qualify anyone for the presidency, any more than Ford's being a graceful dancer. (Betty Ford, a one-time dance professional, would extol her husband's talents on the ballroom floor.)

Yet Ford continued to be spoofed for his clumsiness, and would laugh at those jokes at his expense. In fact, he often contributed to the myth in banter with Bob Hope. Actually, I saw Ford ski at Vail at age 70, an athletic feat few reporters could match. Ford may not have been a glamorous idol like JFK, but the fact that Ford was once the cover boy for *Cosmopolitan* in 1939 was somehow neglected by the Washington press.

To bring to light some of the unappreciated details of Ford's background doesn't mean that he was a complicated personality. The man one saw on television was the real Ford. There was no persona in his image. As one who was adopted by his stepfather, Gerald Ford, Sr. (his birth name was Leslie King), Gerald Ford could have suffered from being abandoned by his real father. But Ford was the least neurotic and best adjusted of any of the five presidents I have known.

In the tape for his autobiography, *A Time to Heal*, he never criticized anybody except former White House Counsel John Dean. Most presidents, if they are not a bit paranoid when they enter the White House, leave feeling a bit persecuted. But unlike most driven politicians, Ford was not insecure. He selected Nelson Rockefeller, whose record in statecraft outshone his own, as his vice president, and kept the brilliant Henry Kissinger as his secretary of state.

As president, he was more accessible than Kennedy and Reagan, and more likable than Nixon and Carter. The overwhelming applause when President Carter singled him out in his inaugural proved his popularity on Capitol Hill on both sides of the aisle.

Ford's popularity forced the beleaguered Nixon to abandon his preference for his secretary of the treasury, John Connolly, to select Ford as vice president. Actually Ford, as the elected leader of Republican congressmen, was the politically proper decision, and so Nixon appointed Ford. A fellow Republican had to succeed the resigned Agnew, who had been re-elected in 1972.

Following President Nixon's resignation, Ford was sworn in on Friday, August 9, 1974. Never before had an accidental presidency been the scene of such a public occasion. It had none of the pomp and pageantry of a scheduled inauguration, but it was very much a public event. Ford himself called old friends like Speaker Tip O'Neill for advice and invited about 300 guests to the ceremony.

To draft his speech, the new president called in Robert T. Hartman, who had spent 25 years at *The Los Angeles Times* before his interest in politics led him to a career as senior aide first to Vice President and then President Ford.

> The oath that I have taken is the same oath that was taken by George Washington. . . . But I assume the Presidency under extraordinary circumstances never before experienced by Americans. This is an hour of history that troubles our minds and hurts our hearts. [1]

Then Ford explained why this would be a different kind of inaugural, adding:

> Not an inaugural address, not a fireside chat, not a campaign speech—just a little straight talk among friends. [. . .] If you have not chosen me by secret ballot, neither have I gained office by any secret promises. I have not cam-

paigned either for the Presidency or the Vice Presidency. I have not subscribed to any partisan platform. I am indebted to no man, and only to one woman, my dear wife—as I begin this very difficult job. [2]

The brusque 59-year-old Hartman was only four years younger than Ford. He was no sycophantic aide, but one who could lay out the brutal facts to Ford. He did not share Ford's admiration for the departing president. He blamed Nixon for the collapse of public trust in government and wanted to immunize his boss from any partisan rancor.

I have not sought this enormous responsibility, but I will not shirk it. Those who nominated and confirmed me as Vice President were my friends and are my friends. They were of both parties, elected by all the people. . . . It is only fitting then that I should pledge to them and to you that I will be the President of all the people. [3]

The speech then buttressed this reliance on the people by quoting the patron saints of both parties: Thomas Jefferson and Abraham Lincoln. Ford then turned to the mid-term elections in the coming fall:

Even though this is late in an election year, there is no way we can go forward except together and no way anybody can win except by serving the people's urgent needs. We cannot stand still or slip backwards. We must go forward now together. [4]

Now Ford came to the much-discussed and re-drafted passage in which he separated himself from Nixon without openly disavowing him.

In all my public and private acts as your President, I expect to follow my instincts of openness and candor with full confidence that honesty is always the best policy in the end. [5]

Then Ford paused to give emphasis to his next sentence.

My fellow Americans, our long national nightmare is over. [6]

Much argument and persuasion were spent in getting Ford to utter "the nightmare phrase." The head of the pragmatic Ford accepted the "nightmare" phrase, but the heart of the longtime loyal political lieutenant at first balked, then gradually came to accept Hartman's judgment.

Ford continued with much worked-over and revised lines thrashed out with Hartman.

Our Constitution works; our great Republic is a government of laws and not of men. Here the people rule. But there is a higher Power, by whatever name we

> honor Him, who ordains not only righteousness but love, not only justice but
> mercy. [7]

Ford, who didn't wear his religion on his sleeve but was a devout Episcopalian, then employed language familiar to a student of the Bible:

> As we bind up the internal wounds of Watergate, more painful and poisonous
> than those of foreign wars, let us restore the Golden Rule to our political
> process, and let brotherly love purge our hearts of suspicion and of hate. [8]

Then the president directed his words to the departed president, whom he
had served with and then under for twenty years.

> In the beginning I asked you to pray for me. Before closing I ask again your
> prayer for Richard Nixon and for his family. [9]

Then Ford added these words to Hartman's:

> May our former President, who brought peace to millions, find it for himself.
> May God bless and comfort his wonderful wife and daughters, whose love and
> loyalty will forever be a shining legacy to all who bear the lonely burdens of
> the White House. [10]

The intrinsic decency of Ford that made him so likable and even loved
was manifest. Ford now closed with this pledge echoing Lincoln's words:

> I now solemnly reaffirm my promise I made to you . . . to uphold the Constitu-
> tion, to do what is right as God gives me to see the right, and to do the very
> best I can for America. God helping me, I will not let you down. Thank you. [11]

The new president's plainspoken words were reminiscent of Harry Truman, whose portrait Ford now installed in the White House. His remarks won
him the good will and high approval of the American people.

A month later, President Ford pardoned former President Nixon. He did
it, he told this writer, not for Nixon's sake but for the country's.

To heal the country, he had to remove Watergate and Nixon from the
daily headlines. He knew, he told this writer, that it would end his political
honeymoon, but it was the only way to begin the healing process.

Years later, Senator Edward Kennedy, who opposed the pardon, admitted
that Ford's decision was courageous as well as correct.

President Ford said to the writers who worked on his memoirs that he
knew it might cost him re-election, but that it was the only way to end the
rancor and recriminations of Watergate and the Nixon presidency and let the
healing process begin.

NOTES

1. Remini and Golway, *Fellow Citizens*, 415.
2. Ibid.
3. Ibid.
4. Ibid., 416.
5. Ibid.
6. Ibid.
7. Ibid.
8. Ibid.
9. Ibid.
10. Ibid.
11. Ibid.

Chapter Eighteen

Jimmy Carter Delivers His "Malaise" Address

In the summer of 1979, President Carter took an urgent phone call from his pollster, Patrick Caddell. This new and untested number-cruncher had once informed him that a Christian evangelist like Carter had a chance of winning the Iowa Caucus vote in 1976. Because caucuses were held at schools, fire stations, and farm houses—not polling stations—they gave an advantage to committed "born-agains" who would drive twenty miles in snowy weather to register their preference.

Governor Carter was already leaning towards a presidential candidacy, but Caddell's analysis was the clincher. In early 1976, Carter pulled off an upset victory in Iowa. Suddenly, Carter jumped from being a presidential curiosity to a Democratic frontrunner. He would garner the nomination and narrowly edge the incumbent president, Gerald Ford.

But now Jimmy Carter was in the White House. A call demanding answers from Caddell, his pollster, did not sound like good news. The former Georgia peanut farmer had capitalized on a singular moment in American political history. After the trauma of Watergate, the country had been ripe for a fresh face—not part of Washington—to lift them from the nadir of the Nixon resignation and South Vietnam's collapse in Asia.

All over the country, Carter had presented himself as a new kind of candidate. He told small groups he met in the election campaign that "I want a government as good as its people." The message registered.

At first, at least symbolically, Carter was something new. At the inaugural he walked down Pennsylvania Avenue—instead of riding in a limousine—and took the time to talk to some of the onlookers. For a while, he didn't fly in Air Force One, but used private commercial planes. When he addressed the country on television, he donned a cardigan, explaining to reporters later that he was saving fuel.

But two years later, a weary president was looking forward to a few days' vacation in Hawaii after a grueling trip to Japan. In his phone call, pollster Caddell said, "Mr. President, you've got to come home now. You have no idea how bad the situation is."

That week the energy crisis that the president had been in since his inauguration had finally turned ugly. OPEC (Organization of the Petroleum Exporting Countries), the oil producers' cartel, had announced another in a series of price increases that had sent prices at the pump skyward. That led to fuel shortages.

A mere speech couldn't quell the rising tempers and frustrations. Instead, Carter announced he was summoning an Economic Summit at Camp David. And he called in an array of economic experts as well as a variety of citizens' groups, including union heads, leaders of African-American groups, farmers, academics, and clergy as well as politicians.

For ten days, a veil of secrecy enveloped the proceedings. Carter had already delivered a series of talks about what should be done on energy.

Caddell had told him that his approval ratings had dipped to 25 percent—lower than Nixon's during Watergate. No more lecturing to the American people—he had to listen to them. So Carter did—hearing harsh complaints, severe criticism, and a host of recommended government measures.

At the end, the president decided he had to deliver an address to the American people.

Carter had written his Inaugural Address without much editorial assistance. But now he turned to writer Rick Herzog, who had been a talented journalist. An admirer of World War II leaders FDR and Churchill, Herzog persuaded the president that we faced a warlike emergency. Herzog seized on one citizen's letter, which said: "Mr. President, we are in trouble. Talk to us about blood and sweat and tears." Another piece of advice that Herzog had read contained the words, "When we enter the moral equivalent of war, don't issue us BB guns."

On July 15, 1979, President Carter delivered his long-awaited speech to the American people.

> Good evening. This is a special night for me. Exactly three years ago, on July 15, 1976, I accepted the nomination of my party to run for President of the United States. I promised you a President who is not isolated from the people, who feels your pain, and who shares your dreams and who draws his strength and wisdom from you. [. . .]
>
> It's clear that the true problems of our Nation are much deeper—deeper than gasoline lines or energy shortages, deeper even than inflation or recession. And I realize more than ever that as President I need your help. So, I decided to reach out and listen to the voices of Americans. [1]

Carter then relayed a litany of criticism, counsel, and advice he had heard: You are not leading this nation; you are only managing the government; don't talk to us about politics or mechanics of government, but about an understanding of our common good. Carter had set up the groundwork for a blunt and candid address—a speech that didn't whitewash facts, nor paint over bad numbers with euphemisms.

> I want to speak to you first tonight about a subject even more serious than energy or inflation. I want to talk to you right now about a fundamental threat to American democracy.[2]

Carter clearly had the attention of his listeners and viewers.

> The threat is nearly invisible in ordinary ways. It is a crisis of confidence. It is a crisis that strikes at the very heart and soul and spirit of our national will. We can see this crisis in the growing doubt about the meaning of our own lives and in the loss of a unity and purpose for our Nation. The erosion of confidence in the future is threatening to destroy the social and the political fabric of America.[3]

The president then explained why confidence in the future is the foundation of our faith.

> Confidence in the future has supported everything else—public institutions and private enterprise, our own families, and the very Constitution of the United States. [. . .]
>   We've always believed in something called progress. We always have had a faith that the days of our children would be better than our own.
>   Our people are losing that faith, not only in government itself but in the ability as citizens to serve as the ultimate rulers and shapers of our democracy. [. . .]
>   The symptoms of this crisis of the American spirit are all around us. For the first time in the history of our country a majority of our people believe that the next five years will be worse than the past five years. Two-thirds of our people do not even vote. The productivity of American workers is actually dropping, and the willingness of Americans to save for the future has fallen below that of all other people in the Western world.[4]

Then, summoning the spirit of Churchill, he proclaims:

> First of all, we must face the truth, and then we can change our course. [. . .]
> One of the visitors to Camp David last week put it this way: "We've got to stop crying and start sweating, stop talking and start walking, stop cursing and start praying. The strength we need will not come from the White House, but from every house in America."[5]

The president then focuses on energy:

> Energy will be the immediate test of our ability to unite this Nation, and it can
> be the standard around which we rally. On the battlefield of energy we can win
> for our Nation a new confidence, and we can seize control again of our com-
> mon destiny. [6]

The president then outlined his steps:

> Point one: . . . cutting our dependence on foreign oil by one-half by the end of
> the next decade. . .
> Point two: . . . to set import quotas. . . .
> Point three: . . . to develop America's own alternative sources of fuel—from
> coal, from oil shale, from plant products for gasohol, from unconventional gas,
> from the Sun.
> Point four: . . . asking Congress to mandate . . . that our Nation's utility
> companies cut their massive use of oil. . . .
> Point five: . . . to create an energy mobilization board. . .
> Point six: . . . proposing a bold conservation program. . . [7]

After outlining his six-point program, Carter reminded his audience that
the future will not be easy:

> I do not promise you that this struggle for freedom will be easy. I do not
> promise a quick way out of our Nation's problems, when the truth is that the
> only way out is an all-out effort. What I do promise you is that I will lead our
> fight, and I will enforce fairness in our struggle, and I will ensure honesty.
> [. . .] There is simply no way to avoid sacrifice. [8]

Then Carter ended:

> In closing, let me say this: I will do my best, but I will not do it alone. Let your
> voice be heard. [. . .] Working together with our common faith we cannot fail.
> Thank you and good night. [9]

The speech was pure Jimmy Carter, a preacher entreating his flock for
greater sacrifice if America is to reach the Promised Land. Rick Herzog had
drafted for the president a Churchillian address laying out the cold facts, then
calling for a war-like resolve to action.

But the American people did not view the energy crisis as equivalent to
World War II, and Jimmy Carter was no such heroic figure as Winston
Churchill.

The Washington press, which had never been warm to the evangelical
preacher, would call it his "Malaise Speech," but Carter never actually used
that word in his talk. Like a biblical prophet, Carter was finding his people
"wanting in spirit."

Yet it was Carter himself who had committed the one unpardonable sin in American politics: He had criticized America and its Americans. The unintended consequences of this turned attention to Carter's own leadership. A week after Carter's address, Senator Ted Kennedy would announce his candidacy. One of the reasons he gave was his deep dismay in a president who would offer despair instead of hope.

NOTES

1. Jimmy Carter, "Crisis of Confidence—Jimmy Carter" (Text of televised address by President Jimmy Carter, July 15, 1979), *WGBH American Experience, PBS Boston,* accessed August 26, 2014, http://www.pbs.org/wgbh/americanexperience/features/primary-resources/carter-crisis/.

2. Ibid.
3. Ibid.
4. Ibid.
5. Ibid.
6. Ibid.
7. Ibid.
8. Ibid.
9. Ibid.

Chapter Nineteen

Ronald Reagan Becomes
the Champion of the Free World

If Abraham Lincoln was the best speechwriter ever to live in the White House, the runner-up was Ronald Reagan. Ronald Reagan was better at turning out a talk than any of his wordsmiths. Invariably, the experience of speechwriters is as journalists writing for the printed page. Reagan, the king of the platform circuit before he ever turned to politics, framed his talks for the ear. Those critics from the left who dismiss his speech success as that of a Hollywood actor who could deliver only from a crafted script are letting their bias cloud their judgment.

In the first place, actors—except for Shakespearian actors such as Laurence Olivier or Richard Burton—do not make eloquent speakers. They are used to a line or two in dialogue but not soliloquies like Hamlet's or orations like Marc Antony's. Yes, Reagan utilized from his acting experience the art of the pause and change of inflection. Reagan, however, gained his mastery at the podium by delivering thousands of addresses to organizations and dinner groups across the nation. These talks were not prepared for him. Just as he crafted his weekly radio talks—for listening audiences—so he carefully issued platform remarks from a series of six-by-eight cards of catchy lines, humorous or poignant anecdotes, and ended with some ringing closers.

He was familiar with the rhetorical bag of tricks of the speechwriters: repetition of words or phrases ("Some years ago the federal government declared war on poverty . . . and poverty won"[1]), internal rhyme ("They have a new kind of layaway plan for your lives which never changes. It's called 'Americans make; government takes'"[2]), or alliteration ("A party platform is a promissory note to the American people that is never paid"[3]), and emotional closers ("You and I have a rendezvous with destiny"[4]).

Reagan also brought to the podium a consummate professionalism never seen in any of his predecessors. This writer sat with him once before he addressed an association of eight hundred listeners. He would not touch his dinner. Beforehand, he had served to him a pot of hot water with lemon, and a chocolate chip cookie wrapped in foil. "I learned this," he told me, "from an old preacher friend (Billy Graham) and crooner pal (Frank Sinatra) to soothe and strengthen the vocal chords." The cookie was for energy. "Never drink caffeine," he advised me, "either in coffee or in Coca Cola; it dehydrates one." Finally, he gave me this strange suggestion: "Always put on a fresh pair of shoes when you are about to talk. It gives you a lift in energy."[5]

One who was a professional even to his shoe-tips needed no coach in delivery. One could learn by watching his television talks—no words ever emanated from his mouth when his eyes were looking downward at notes. He would pause and his eyes would photograph the phrase before him and then deliver it with his eyes straight into the camera. Few are the speakers who master this art of never looking down at their text while speaking.

But for all his mastery of speech delivery, he still needed assistance in speech preparation. The time demands were too overwhelming to carry out the research needed for a major address.

Ken Khachigian, a California writer who had penned speeches for Nixon, drafted Reagan's First Inaugural Address. He caught the muscular prose of Reagan: "We are a nation that has a government—not the other way around . . . it's not my intention to do away with government. It is rather to make it work."[6]

The inaugural is usually the supreme challenge to a new president, but for Reagan it was his 1982 speech at the Palace of Westminster in London. His political soul mate, Prime Minister Margaret Thatcher, had invited Reagan to speak—a singular honor never extended to any previous president.

To write this address, Reagan chose a movement conservative, Tony Dolan. Dolan saw in the upcoming London address a history-in-the-making parallel with Churchill's "Iron Curtain" address to America in 1946.

Yet if Churchill called for the containment of Communism, Dolan thought Reagan should stress a "Crusade for Freedom."

In May, Dolan submitted his draft to his superior, Dave Gergen, the head of the White House "Communications Shop." Gergen, who had written for both Nixon and Ford, thought Dolan, the right-wing polemicist, too hard-edged for a European audience, who imagined Reagan as a kind of John Wayne, a cowboy-actor—too fast on the draw. But Dolan, anticipating such a reaction, had back-channeled it to Reagan. Reagan read the draft and saw in it something he had been wanting to say in his role as Leader of the Free World. Curiously, although Reagan regarded speeches as a prime requisite of leadership, he did not enjoy a close relationship with his writers, as Kennedy had with Ted Sorensen or Nixon with Ray Price.

Unlike Kennedy or Nixon, Reagan practiced his speeches aloud. If Nixon in his many drafts of a speech would edit every nuance for substance, Reagan would re-write an address for reasons of style.

He opened:

> Speaking for all Americans, I want to say how much at home we feel in your house. Every American would, because this is, as we have been so eloquently told, one of democracy's shrines.[7]

Dolan then had Reagan come to the theme of the address by citing British Prime Minister Gladstone with respect to the developing "Solidarity Movement" in Poland.

> "You cannot fight against the future. Time is on our side."[8]

Reagan followed:

> Optimism is in order, because day by day democracy is proving itself to be a not-at-all fragile flower.[9]

The next line was a deliberate attempt by Dolan to echo the "Iron Curtain" lines of Churchill:

> From Stettin on the Baltic to Varna on the Black Sea, the regimes planted by totalitarianism have had more than thirty years to establish their legitimacy. But none—not one regime—has yet been able to risk free elections.[10]

Dolan had Reagan summarize with an alliterative aphorism:

> Regimes planted by bayonets do not take root.[11]

Reagan then added to Dolan's draft a Churchill bon mot about John Foster Dulles. It alluded to the often-heavy hand of American diplomacy.

> Sir Winston Churchill said in exasperation about one of our most distinguished diplomats: "He is the only case I know of a bull who carries his china shop with him."[12]

Reagan's audience roared with delight. The self-deprecation that is a trade-mark of British as well as Reagan humor won the hearts of even those on the Labour side who regarded Reagan's right-wing philosophy as even more unpalatable than Thatcher's.

The light note turned somber as Reagan noted:

It was not the democracies that invaded Afghanistan or suppressed Polish
Solidarity or used chemical and toxin warfare in Afghanistan and Southeast
Asia. [13]

For Reagan's reaction to Soviet aggression, Dolan would then borrow the
stately cadences of Churchill:

If history teaches us anything, it teaches self-delusion in the face of unpleasant
facts is folly. [14]

Reagan then asks rhetorically:

What, then, is our course? Must civilization perish in a hail of fiery atoms?
Must freedom wither in a quiet, deadening accommodation with totalitarian
evil? [15]

For his answer, Dolan would have Reagan quote Churchill's "Iron Curtain"
speech:

"I do not believe that Soviet Russia desires war. What they desire is the fruits
of war and the indefinite expansion of their power and doctrines. . . . " [16]

Reagan then called for a plan that was a prophecy:

What I am describing now is a plan and a hope for the long term—the march
of freedom and democracy which will leave Marxism–Leninism on the ash-
heap of history . . . the struggle that's now going on in the world will not be
bombs and rockets, but a test of wills and ideas, a trial of spiritual resolve, the
values we hold, the beliefs we cherish, the ideals to which we are dedicated. [17]

The voice was Reagan's but it sounded Churchillian. Reagan would close
with this peroration:

Let us now begin a major effort to secure the best—a crusade for freedom that
will engage the faith and fortitude of the next generation. [18]

For major addresses, Reagan would continue to draw from the intellectual
right wing for drafts. George Gilder, a philosopher from the ranks of the New
Right, would write Reagan's noteworthy speech to Moscow University.

Reagan's favorite writer was the lyrical Peggy Noonan, who would pen
his more poignant odes—such as when the Space Shuttle *Challenger* ex-
ploded.

We shall never forget them, nor the last time we saw them, this morning, as
they prepared for their journey and waved good-bye and "slipped the surly
bonds of earth" to "touch the face of God." [19]

Yet Reagan's supreme address as Leader of the Free World had been to the Palace of Westminster in 1982, when Tony Dolan helped drape the mantle of Churchill around Reagan to prophesy the end of Communism.

As I wrote before, Reagan did not talk speech points with his writers. But he still made sure that his speeches bore his own imprint. The most remembered of his lines are those he uttered in June 1987 in Berlin. That rhetorical challenge was given to writer Peter Hannaford, an advertising executive Reagan had known since his Sacramento days. Three times Reagan inserted into the text the remarks he would utter at the Berlin Wall. Three times State Department bureaucrats crossed out the words as too provocative in the tense Cold War.

But at the time of the talk, Reagan winked at Hannaford and did a thumbs-up:

> General Secretary Gorbachev, if you seek peace, if you seek prosperity for the Soviet Union and Eastern Europe, if you seek liberalization: Come here to this gate! Mr. Gorbachev, open this gate! Mr. Gorbachev, tear down this wall![20]

Hannaford told me later he thought the State Department types would wet their striped pants!

NOTES

1. Ronald Reagan, "Address Before a Joint Session of Congress on the State of the Union, January 25, 1988," John T. Woolley and Gerhard Peters, eds., *The American Presidency Project, University of California, Santa Barbara,* accessed July 30, 2015, http://www.presidency.ucsb.edu/ws/?pid=36035.

2. Ronald Reagan, "Remarks at the National Conference of the National Federation of Independent Business" (Washington, D.C., June 22, 1983), *The University of Texas Archives, Ronald Reagan Presidential Library,* accessed July 31, 2015, http://www.reagan.utexas.edu/archives/speeches/1983/62283b.htm.

3. James C. Humes, *The Reagan Persuasion: Charm, Deliver and Inspire a Winning Message* (Naperville, IL: Sourcebooks, Inc., 2010), 57.

4. Ronald Reagan, "Address on Behalf of Senator Barry Goldwater: 'Rendezvous with Destiny,' October 27, 1964," *AMDOCS: Documents for the Study of American History,* accessed August 1, 2015, http://www.vlib.us/amdocs/texts/reagan101964.html.

5. Humes, *The Reagan Persuasion,* 120.

6. Ronald Reagan, "Ronald Reagan: Inaugural Address, January 20, 1981," John T. Woolley and Gerhard Peters, eds., *The American Presidency Project, University of California, Santa Barbara,* accessed August 2, 2015, http://www.presidency.ucsb.edu/ws/?pid=43130.

7. Humes, *My Fellow Americans,* 267.

8. Ibid.

9. Ibid.

10. Ibid.

11. Ibid.

12. Ibid., 268.

13. Ibid.

14. Ibid.

15. Ibid.

16. Ibid.

17. Ibid., 270.

18. Ibid., 271.

19. Ronald Reagan, "The History Place — Great Speeches Collection: Ronald Reagan Speech on the Space Shuttle Challenger" (Televised address to the nation on the Challenger Disaster, January 28, 1986, alluding to John Gillespie Magee's poem, "High Flight"), *The History Place*[TM], accessed August 20, 2014, http://www.historyplace.com/speeches/reagan-challenger.htm.

20. Romesh Ratnesar, *Tear Down This Wall: A City, a President, and the Speech that Ended the Cold War* (New York: Simon and Schuster, 2009), 210.

Chapter Twenty

George H.W. Bush Delivers
His Kinder and Gentler Inaugural

If by presidential qualifications, we mean actual experience, George H.W. Bush is the most qualified person ever to run for the nation's highest office. Bush had been congressman, ambassador to the United Nations, director of the CIA, and envoy to China. As a bonus, Bush could claim a Phi Beta Kappa from Yale and was selected a College All-American First Baseman.

Bush had run for the GOP presidential nomination in 1980 against Governor Reagan. But unfortunately for him, the moderate Eastern wing of the Party had atrophied. Since 1964 the base of the Party was right wing. Bush's hope was that he would be seen as a sure-fire winner against the Democrats, whereas Reagan's hopes were problematic—possibly too reactionary for independents and moderates.

In the early Iowa caucus, Bush upset favorite Reagan. Bush bragged about the momentum, or "The Big Mo," as he called it in the New Hampshire primary. "The Big Mo" was a code word for sure winner in November.

But in the New Hampshire debate between all the GOP candidates—which Reagan had funded—the media maestro won the debate, and probably the nomination, with his comment, "I am paying for this microphone, Mr. Green." [1]

For the rest of the primary season, Bush tried to play catch-up with the hope that Reagan might choose him to be his running mate.

But at the Detroit Convention, Henry Kissinger exploited Reagan's initial dislike of Bush to try to broker a Reagan–Ford ticket. At first the former president was amenable, but Kissinger's pushing Ford to demand a primary role for himself in foreign policy sank any possibility of this.

So Bush, who had already packed his bags to return to Texas, was then chosen as Reagan's V.P. Polls showed he was the only Republican—besides

Ford—who would add voting appeal for the Eastern states. The combination would overwhelm Carter and Mondale in the election.

The new president's relations with his vice president were cordial and correct, but not close. Yet Bush proved to be a loyal and effective vice president for two terms and a front-runner for the nomination in 1988. (Interestingly, Reagan in 1988 like Eisenhower in 1960 would have run for a third term if the Constitutional amendment barring a third term hadn't passed in 1953. It was the GOP's posthumous revenge against FDR, but it may have backfired.)

Bush had no special regard for speechwriters. He didn't share Reagan's belief that leadership was eighty percent communication. He once told this writer, "Most speeches are B.S." It probably stemmed from his patrician distaste for boasting about oneself or one's achievements. He once deleted from this writer's work an account of his Navy plane being shot down into the Pacific.

Bush tried in vain to talk more like a "movement conservative," but the Reaganites never learned to love him. He won with the aid of speechwriter Peggy Noonan's line, "Read my lips: No new taxes."[2]

By 1988, former Nixon communications advisor Roger Ailes urged him to hire Peggy Noonan. In doing so, Bush didn't choose a movement conservative like Tony Dolan or George Gilder, but one who was more noted for her lyrical than her ideological pen.

Bush beat Massachusetts Governor Michael Dukakis. One line from the debate summed it up. When the Democratic candidate attacked Bush for Iran Contra, Bush replied, "I will take the blame for these two incidents [Noriega and Iran Contra] if you give me half the credit for all the good things that have happened in world peace since Ronald Reagan and I took over from the Carter administration."[3] The voters gave credit where credit was due, and so Bush won. But it was actually a vote for a third term for Reagan.

Any speechwriter for Bush had a hard time finding out Bush's dreams for the future or his doctrines for doing so. Bush was a patriot, an Episcopalian, and a Republican, but that was it. And that was the beginning and end of his political philosophy. The same might be said of another George—our first president. Both, however, had this in common—duty. Bush had like Washington a patrician sense of noblesse oblige.

Peggy Noonan was born in Brooklyn. She came from the Irish American working class who found a hero in Ronald Reagan for making "patriotism" not a pejorative. For many children and grandchildren of immigrants, the exceptionalism of America was no fable. It was fact and Reagan was unapologetic about reaffirming it.

Noonan's love of American heroes was manifest in her two moving and poignant tributes for Reagan, at D-Day's Normandy Beach and for the Space Shuttle *Challenger* disaster.

The chemistry between the patrician Yalie and the journalism graduate from Farleigh-Dickinson in New York was not ideal. If Bush never was known for working well with his speechwriters, he also never interfered by editing or rewriting their work. He was also not known for discussing any vision with them. "Vision," he once told this writer, "leave that to the dreamers or poets." He did, however, want Noonan to draft a speech that would both satisfy Reaganites and also signal to the loyal Bushites, who had been out of favor with movement conservatives. Noonan would do this by emphasizing the word "new" in the talk—"new breeze," three times; "new engagement," twice; "new ground" and "new action," once.

For his inaugural, President Bush—at Ailes' demand—would rehearse this speech as he had his acceptance speech at the GOP convention in August. Peggy Noonan would begin the address by taking special note of Bush's predecessor.

Bush would open:

> There is a man here who has earned a lasting place in our hearts and in our history. President Reagan, on behalf of our Nation, I thank you for the wonderful things that you have done for America.[4]

Then Bush really began his address:

> We meet on democracy's front porch, a good place to talk as neighbors and friends. For this is a day when our nation is made whole, when our differences, for a moment, are suspended. [. . .] I come before you and assume the Presidency at a moment rich with promise. We live in a peaceful, prosperous time, but we can make it better.[5]

Here Noonan had Bush utter a quartet of "new's," stressed by alliteration and emphasized by repetition, and then in a metaphor for dying Communism, another alliteration:

> For a new breeze is blowing, and a world refreshed by freedom seems reborn; for in man's heart, if not in fact, the day of the dictator is over. The totalitarian era is passing, its old ideas blown away like leaves from an ancient, lifeless tree. A new breeze is blowing, and a nation refreshed by freedom stands ready to push on. There is new ground to be broken, and new action to be taken. There are times when the future seems thick as a fog; you sit and wait, hoping the mists will lift and reveal the right path. But this is a time when the future seems a door you can walk right through into a room called tomorrow.[6]

Bush continued with Noonan's door-opening metaphor:

> Great nations of the world are moving toward democracy through the door to freedom. Men and women of the world move towards free markets through the

door to prosperity. The people of the world agitate for free expression and free thought through the door to the moral and intellectual satisfaction that only liberty allows. [7]

Bush then extolled freedom:

> We know what works: Freedom works. We know what's right: Freedom is right. We know how to secure a more just and prosperous life for man on Earth: through free markets, free speech, free elections, and the exercise of free will unhampered by the state. [8]

Then Noonan wrote what Bush asked her to stress: his compassionate conservative side, which his predecessor never stressed.

> No President, no government, can teach us to remember what is best in what we are. But if the man you have chosen to lead this government can help make a difference; if he can celebrate the quieter, deeper successes that are made not of gold and silk, but of better hearts and finer souls; if he can do these things, then he must. [9]

Then Noonan had Bush introduce the line that rubbed some Reaganites' sensitivities raw:

> America is never wholly herself unless she is engaged in high moral principle. We as a people have such a purpose today. It is to make kinder the face of the Nation and gentler the face of the world. [10]

Bush then listed some of these problems of poverty: the homeless, the children who have nothing, the drug-addicted and crime-afflicted. He continued:

> The old solution, the old way, was to think public money alone could end these problems. But we have learned that is not so. And in any case, our funds are low. We have a deficit to bring down. We have more will than wallet; but will is what we need. [. . .]
> I am speaking of a new engagement in the lives of others, a new activism, hands-on and involved, that gets the job done. [11]

Here Noonan stressed the true colors of the noblesse oblige Bush—the community activist, the civic leader, the patron of the United Negro College Fund:

> I have spoken of a thousand points of light, of all the community organizations that are spread like stars throughout the Nation, doing good. [. . .] The old ideas are new again because they are not old, they are timeless: duty, sacrifice, commitment, and a patriotism that finds its expression in taking part and pitching in. [. . .]
> Our children are watching in schools throughout our great land. And to them I say, thank you for watching democracy's big day. For democracy

belongs to us all, and freedom is like a big kite that can go higher and higher with the breeze. [. . .] A President is neither prince nor pope, and I don't seek a window on men's souls. In fact, I yearn for a greater tolerance, an easy-goingness about each other's attitudes and way of life. [12]

That was a clear signal to the religious right to mute their sharp rhetoric. And Bush closed not in a dramatic summons, but rather an earnest entreaty.

Some see leadership as high drama, and the sounds of trumpets calling, and sometimes it is that. But I see history as a book with many pages, and each day we fill a page with acts of hopefulness and meaning. The new breeze blows, a page turns, the story unfolds. And so today a chapter begins, a small and stately story of unity, diversity, and generosity—shared, and written, together.

Thank you. God bless you and God bless the United States of America. [13]

Bush had completed the greatest speech he ever delivered. The former college baseball star hit a home run. He had practiced hard on it. He was no orator like Reagan, but on that day, his inaugural excelled.

On that day, Bush revealed the man that his legion of followers knew from school, the service, politics, and businesses, a man of utter decency who was always guided by duty.

NOTES

1. George H.W. Bush, "'I Paid for This Microphone': The Reagan v. Bush Debate Controversy" (Debate among Republican Presidential Candidates, Nashua, New Hampshire, February 23, 1980), *NBC Learn K-12 Website, NBCUniversal Media, LLC,* accessed July 4, 2015, https://archives.nbclearn.com/portal/site/k-12/browse/?cuecard=4511.

2. George H.W. Bush, "Address Accepting the Presidential Nomination at the Republican National Convention in New Orleans, August 18, 1988," John T. Woolley and Gerhard Peters, eds., *The American Presidency Project, University of California, Santa Barbara,* accessed July 4, 2015, http://www.presidency.ucsb.edu/ws/?pid=25955.

3. George H.W. Bush, "Debate with Michael Dukakis, September 25, 1988" (Winston-Salem, North Carolina), *The Miller Center, University of Virginia,* accessed July 4, 2015, http://millercenter.org/president/bush/speeches/speech-5527.

4. Remini and Golway, *Fellow Citizens,* 443.

5. Ibid., 444.

6. Ibid.

7. Ibid.

8. Ibid.

9. Ibid., 445.

10. Ibid.

11. Ibid., 445–446.

12. Ibid., 446–447.

13. Ibid., 448.

Chapter Twenty-One

Bill Clinton Manifests Communication Magic in Oklahoma

Bill Clinton can manifest small-audience magic. But of the many political skills Bill Clinton brought to the White House, that of orator or inspirational platform speaker was not one of them. Clinton bombed in his first debut on the national stage in 1988, at the Democratic National Convention in Atlanta, when the then-Arkansas governor delivered the keynote speech at the request of Governor Dukakis, the Democratic presidential nominee. His two inaugural addresses were flat also. If compared to his hero John F. Kennedy's memorable eloquence in delivering his address, it was a failure.

It is noteworthy that, considering Bill Clinton's unquestionable popularity, not one of his quotations or catchy phrases passed into the vernacular—except possibly "It's the economy, stupid"—in the campaign of 1992, or the definition of "is" in his impeachment ordeal.

This writer does not mean to imply that Bill Clinton lacked communication gifts. At close range in small audiences, at a White House Rose Garden presentation, or for a gathering in the Oval Office, Bill Clinton was captivating. His open and accessible personality was part of it. It was an outward warmth that became almost tangible through his gestures and facial mobility.

Many to whom this writer spoke later told me they would encounter Clinton a skeptic and exit a believer. Tom Kean, former governor of New Jersey, who handled the senior Bush's campaign in the Garden State, said after the two of them had lunch together, "It was as if we shared so many common ideas about everything." (Yet, after Clinton left the presidency, Kean would comment after a meeting, "You couldn't get him to stop talking.")

Clinton was the consummate seducer. Clinton had the compulsion to make everyone his friend and he usually succeeded.

But when you put him in the Oval Office with television cameras trained on him, his power of personality failed to translate to television. His charisma never seemed to surface on formally staged occasions.

The Greek God Antaeus was a giant who lost his strength when his feet weren't touching the ground. Clinton's magnetic power disappeared if his audience was not in almost tactile reach. If he could engage each of their faces as he spoke, however, Clinton was matchless.

In his White House meetings with reporters, Clinton surpassed every recent president but FDR and JFK. These two might have excelled Clinton in wit but not in brains.

Clinton's intuitive intelligence approached brilliance. If he was not the brightest ever to inhabit the Oval Office, he was close to it. That mind plus his fierce ambition would propel him to the Democratic nomination and later to beat the popular incumbent George H.W. Bush.

Aided by the slackening economy and the third-party candidacy of billionaire Ross Perot, Clinton managed to beat both the elder Bush in 1992 and Senator Dole in 1996. In both cases he was more likable. Clinton—whatever his failings in private life—was a dynamic candidate. Some found his "Peck's bad boy" image sexy. If he wasn't as good-looking as JFK, he was just as sensuous if not more so to audiences.

Of all the recent presidents, Clinton was the most secretive about his speechwriters. The golfer who sometimes would cheat on his round cards was once seen in Air Force One rewriting a text in his own handwriting to suggest that he crafted his own speeches. Actually, in short presentations or dedication remarks, Clinton had more impact when he winged it. Usually for short remarks, Clinton would memorize the gist and then deliver it without notes.

But those talks when reported in the press never read as well on paper as they sounded to his listeners. Clinton's vibrancy, charisma, and mobility of expression didn't translate well on the printed page.

The address that most Clinton devotees would call his most poignant was his speech at the Oklahoma State Fair Arena in Oklahoma City in April 1995. Unlike an inaugural, it did not require him to be boxed in far from the audience. Nor was he speaking to fellow politicians, as in a State of the Union Address.

An Arkansan, he knew his neighbor Oklahomans. He was also familiar with their state fair. Although it was not widely reported, he did utilize the speechwriting talents of Michael Waldman. Waldman, a graduate of Columbia University and NYU law school, was a polished writer.

The president read the draft by Waldman, and memorized much of it by reading it aloud in the Oval Office. After thanking the workers and volunteers, Clinton began:

We pledge to do all we can to help you heal the injured, to rebuild this city, and to bring to justice those who did this evil. [1]

No president was better by voice, inflection, and gesture in sharing group pain.

And to all the members of the families here present who have suffered loss—though we share your grief, your pain is unimaginable, and we know that. We cannot undo it. That is God's work. [2]

The president paused to survey some of the sea of faces in front of him, and cited the words of a young widow whose husband had been killed in the downing of Pan Am 103:

The anger you feel is valid, but you must not allow yourselves to be consumed by it. The hurt you feel must not be allowed to turn into hate, but instead into the search for justice. The loss you feel must not paralyze your own lives. Instead, you must try to pay tribute to your loved ones by continuing to do all the things they left undone, thus ensuring they did not die in vain. [. . .]

You have lost too much, but you have not lost everything. And you have certainly not lost America, for we will stand with you for as many tomorrows as it takes. [. . .]

To all my fellow Americans beyond this hall, I say, one thing we owe those who have sacrificed is the duty to purge ourselves of the dark forces which gave rise to this evil. They are forces that threaten our common peace, our freedom, our way of life. [3]

Clinton knew he was addressing church-going people. He had sung and prayed with similar people in Arkansas pews. So his words would be the words of the scripture, familiar to his audience.

Let us teach our children that the God of comfort is also the God of righteousness. Those who trouble their own house will inherit the wind. Justice will prevail. [4]

The Elizabethan majesty of the King James Bible is then heard:

Let us let our own children know that we will stand against the forces of fear. When there is talk of hatred, let us stand up and talk against it. When there is talk of violence, let us stand up and talk against it. In the face of deceit, let us honor life. As St. Paul admonished us, let us not be overcome by evil, but overcome evil with good. [5]

Clinton then shared a story that he and his wife, Hillary, had heard from the daughter of one of the Alfred P. Murrah Building's federal employees:

She said we should all plant a tree in memory of the children. So this morning before we got on the plane to come here, at the White House, we planted that tree in honor of the children of Oklahoma.

It was a dogwood with its wonderful spring flower and its deep, enduring roots. It embodies the lesson of the Psalms—that a life of a good person is like a tree whose leaf does not wither.[6]

Clinton ended on this poignant note:

My fellow Americans, a tree takes a long time to grow, and wounds take a long time to heal. But we must begin. Those who are lost now belong to God. Some day we will be with them. But until that happens, their legacy must be our lives.

Thank you all, and God bless you.[7]

The crowd in the Oklahoma City Hall did not cheer, they cried. With phrases and words so familiar to church-attending Oklahomans, Clinton offered healing words for wounded souls.

Clinton may have a few blemishes in his character, but there are no flaws in his heart, which he wears on his sleeve. His journey from the piney woods of Arkansas to the river of the Potomac was an impossible dream that he fulfilled.

His record as president was mixed. His most substantive achievements were the North Atlantic Trade Accords and reform of the welfare work laws. Both had been Republican initiatives and endorsed by President George H.W. Bush.

It is noteworthy that the boy who grew up essentially fatherless would find his father figure in the man he defeated; that man's name was Bush.

NOTES

1. William Jefferson Clinton, "American Rhetoric: William Jefferson Clinton—Oklahoma Bombing Memorial Prayer Service Address, April 23, 1995," *American Rhetoric, Top 100 Speeches,* accessed August 27, 2014, http://www.americanrhetoric.com/speeches/wjcoklahom-abombingspeech.htm.
2. Ibid.
3. Ibid.
4. Ibid.
5. Ibid.
6. Ibid.
7. Ibid.

Chapter Twenty-Two

The Second Bush Issue — A Historic Summons to the Free World

Both George Bush I and George Bush II seem, at first glance, to come from the same mold. Both prepped at Andover and graduated from Yale. In addition, the two shared a passion for the American national pastime—baseball. (The father was All-American first baseman for Yale and the son a middling Little League catcher for Midland, Texas.)

The senior Bush amassed his experience in foreign policy and national security—UN ambassador, CIA director, and envoy to China. The younger Bush's entire governmental career was in Texas as governor.

Governor Ann Richards, whom George W. Bush defeated, said disparagingly of young Bush's credentials, "He started out at third base thinking he had hit a triple." But Bush proved to be a resourceful and hard-hitting candidate, and won the presidency. Bush, however, had two huge assets.

He bore a name that was a nationally known and respected brand, and he was a Texan, a big state in electoral votes. He had won two elections in Texas. As chief executive of one of the largest states in the Union, he was instantly the leading GOP candidate. Senator John McCain may have been popular with independents and some sections of the media, but in the end he was no match for the Bush national network of money-givers.

This writer came to know George W. in 1987 when he was assisting his father in his presidential run. If he had a more infectious likeability than his more reserved father, it never occurred to me that he was a future president. Our conversation mostly consisted of Churchill anecdotes and baseball statistics.

Despite rumors to the contrary, Bush Senior never offered advice to his son except when his counsel was sought. But a report that circulated had some truth in it. The family generally agreed that Jeb Bush, the Florida candidate for governor in the same year George W. was running against Richards, was superior to George in governmental skills and knowledge. When Jeb lost narrowly to Lawton Childs, the family favorite became W.

If George W. was not the family black sheep, he certainly had his own way of doing things. Like Amos Kendall, the Dartmouth one-time protégé of Whig Henry Clay, who became a gun-toting, Western-hat-wearing convert to frontier Jacksonianism, George W. in his youth picked a set of rambunctious friends who swore, chewed tobacco, and drank hard. By the time W. ran for governor, his Methodist wife, Laura, had put an end to his drinking. Once nominally Episcopalian like his parents, he became a born-again Christian.

In 2000, he faced Clinton's vice president, Al Gore, in one of the nation's closest elections. Like Vice President Nixon in 1960, Gore won the popular vote. (In Nixon's case, if the votes of the Southern states of Georgia, Alabama, and Mississippi that voted for Dixiecrats were subtracted, Nixon would have narrowly won.) But Gore would lose the electoral vote of the deciding state, Florida. (Here, the younger Bush called on Jim Baker, his father's secretary of state, to handle the vote controversy. The Supreme Court was the final arbiter and Bush won.)

Bush did not consult his father's advice to choose his running mate. Dick Cheney from Wyoming added no electoral advantage. But Bush had seen the mistakes of his father and Nixon in not weighing the importance of "gravitas." Senator Dan Quayle and Governor Spiro Agnew had cost Republican votes in the election.

Bush was determined to pick a running mate who added strength to his vulnerability in foreign policy experience. Strange to say—considering the later animus the press would develop against Cheney—the mainstream media generally applauded Bush's choice.

In another respect, too, Bush, unlike his father, realized his utterances would shape the public reaction to him. The senior Bush's choice of Peggy Noonan was his singular exception. The elder Bush never put much stock in his writers and didn't utilize them for the most part.

W. speechwriter Michael Gerson was more than a skilled wordsmith; he would wield some influence in foreign policy. In college at Georgetown, he had switched to Wheaton College in Illinois, the school of Billy Graham. In his epiphany, he became a fervent Evangelist. In these views, he bonded with George W. in his position on Israel.

W., unlike his father, had become a born-again Christian and a new kind of conservative. In a bow to defense and foreign policy, the younger Bush appointed General Colin Powell to be his secretary of state, to confirm his "Compassionate Conservative" appeal to centrists.

As secretary of defense, he appointed the steel-edged Donald Rumsfeld, who was no friend of his father's. Young Bush supplemented his appointment of Rumsfeld with his selection of Michael Gerson as his speechwriter. Gerson was a hardliner on Middle East matters.

In January 2001, when Bush took his oath, the world was at peace and America was prosperous. But politically the country was recovering from a bitter campaign. Only weeks earlier in December, the Supreme Court had ended the recount and gave the presidency to Bush.

For this inaugural address, Bush told Gerson he must cool the fires of partisanship first and then present him as a "Compassionate Conservative." Gore in his campaign had the difficult task of being heir to a popular president who had been impeached. Gore had almost succeeded.

Bush opened his address in a placating gesture, praising both Clinton for "his service to the nation" and Vice President Gore "for a contest conducted with spirit" and "with grace." It was a study in contrast, given its broad appeal to both liberals and conservatives.

> We have a place, all of us, in a long story—a story we continue, but whose end we will not see. It is a story of a new world that became a friend and liberator of the old, a story of a slave-holding society that became a servant of freedom, the story of a power that went into the world to protect but not possess, to defend but not to conquer. It is the American story. . . . [1]

Gerson in the address would feature the president as a compassionate conservative by employing the words "compassion" three times and "compassionate" once. Clearly Gerson was fashioning the new president as something other than an ideological right-winger. In the address, Gerson would hint at the direction in which Bush would apply his compassionate philosophy to national problems.

> The ambitions of some Americans are limited by failing schools and hidden prejudices and the circumstances of their birth. [2]

This was an implied promise of his "No Child Left Behind" initiative, which he had earlier joined with Senator Edward Kennedy to propose. Bush had a progressive record as Texas governor, in reforming education and trimming the trial attorneys' agenda with a tort reform bill he had enacted.

But Bush's presidency was fated to be remembered not for any domestic achievements, but for his security measures as Commander-in-Chief. This was in reaction to the terrorist attacks in September 2001 that killed more than three thousand people, brought down the World Trade Center in Manhattan, and damaged a portion of the Pentagon.

The attacks of 9/11 rallied the country behind President Bush. A U.S.-led international coalition countered any Afghan threat. Victory there emboldened the Bush administration to invade Iraq, where dictator Saddam Hussein reportedly had weapons of mass destruction. In the ensuing conflict, Hussein was driven from power. He was later captured and executed by the new Iraqi government, although the WMDs— reported by both British and U.S. intelligence—were never located.

But by the campaign season of 2004, the rejoicing at victory had been succeeded by a rancor caused by a bloody occupation. The U.S.-led coalition forces were challenged by Hussein's private militias and loosely organized guerillas.

Sensing Bush's vulnerability, the Democrats nominated John Kerry, a Senator and a Vietnam veteran who had turned against the Vietnam War.

While Kerry focused on the quagmire in Iraq, Bush asked for patience in the global war against terror. His plea that he kept the country safe from another terrorist attack was persuasive.

Whether Bush's decision to invade Iraq was right will be determined by history. If Iraq develops into a viable representative government in the Middle East, Bush will find himself vindicated.

For this Second Inaugural Address, Bush would summon a united Free World against the global terrorism of Jihad. In his opening remarks, Bush stated:

> At this second gathering, our duties are defined not by the words I use, but by the history we have seen together. For half a century, America defended our own freedom by standing watch on distant borders. After the shipwreck of communism came years of relative quiet, years of repose, years of sabbatical—and then there came a day of fire.[3]

Michael Gerson was more than a phrasemaker in this address; he was also in part a policy-maker. Gerson was a neo-con and a strong advocate for the invasion to oust a fascist dictator, Hussein of Iraq.

> We have seen our vulnerability—and we have seen its deepest source. For as long as whole regions of the world simmer in resentment and tyranny—prone to ideologies that feed hatred and excuse murder—violence will gather, and multiply in destructive power, and cross the most defended borders, and raise a mortal threat.[4]

Bush then asserted that there is only one way to stop this scourge.

> There is only one force of history that can break the reign of hatred and resentment, and expose the pretensions of tyrants, and reward the hopes of the decent and tolerant, and that is the force of human freedom.[5]

Bush expanded upon this theme.

> We are led, by events and common sense, to one conclusion: The survival of liberty in our land increasingly depends on the success of liberty in other lands.

The best hope for peace in our world is the expansion of freedom in all the world.[6]

The Christian Gerson had his fellow Christian believer Bush assert the presence of God, and then followed it with a line from Lincoln.

From the day of our Founding, we have proclaimed that every man and woman on this earth has rights, and dignity, and matchless value, because they bear the image of the Maker of Heaven and Earth. Across the generations we have proclaimed the imperative of self-government, because no one is fit to be a master, and no one deserves to be a slave.[7]

Bush now came to his central theme.

My most solemn duty is to protect this nation and its people against further attacks and emerging threats. Some have unwisely chosen to test America's resolve, and have found it firm.[8]

Bush continued his pledge.

We will persistently clarify the choice before every ruler and every nation: The moral choice between oppression, which is always wrong, and freedom, which is eternally right. America will not pretend that jailed dissidents prefer their chains, or that women welcome humiliation and servitude, or that any human being aspires to live at the mercy of bullies.[9]

This was a stern warning to the Axis of Evil, which Gerson had identified as North Korea and Iran together with Iraq.

Bush then described the adversary.

The rulers of outlaw regimes can know that we still believe as Abraham Lincoln did: "Those who deny freedom to others deserve it not for themselves; and, under the rule of a just God, cannot long retain it."[10]

Bush again had invoked the liberating spirit of Lincoln's Gettysburg Address and Second Inaugural.

Our country has accepted obligations that are difficult to fulfill, and would be dishonorable to abandon. Yet because we have acted in the great liberating tradition of this nation, tens of millions have achieved their freedom. And as hope kindles hope, millions more will find it. By our efforts, we have lit a fire as well—a fire in the minds of men. It warms those who feel its power; it burns those who fight its progress, and one day this untamed fire of freedom will reach the darkest corners of our world. [. . .]

America has need of idealism and courage, because we have essential work at home—the unfinished work of American freedom. In a world moving

toward liberty, we are determined to show the meaning and promise of liberty.[11]

Bush would then stress that the war against terror was not a fight against
Islam.

> In America's ideal of freedom, the public depends on private character—
> integrity and tolerance towards others and the role of conscience in our own
> life. . . . That character is built in families supported by communities with
> standards and sustained in our national life by the truth of lines from the
> Sermon on the Mount and the Koran.[12]

Bush continued to echo Lincoln's compassion for the poor and dispossessed.

> In America's ideal of freedom, the exercise of rights is ennobled by service,
> and mercy, and a heart for the weak. [. . .] Our nation relies on men and
> women who look after a neighbor and surround the lost with love. . . . [we]
> must always remember that even the unwanted have worth. And our country
> must abandon all the habits of racism, because we cannot carry the message of
> freedom and the baggage of bigotry at the same time.[13]

The internal rhyme and alliteration at the last line triggered applause.
Bush drew his remarks to a close with this expression of faith in freedom:

> We go forward with complete confidence in the eventual triumph of freedom.
> Not because history runs on the wheels of inevitability; it is human choices
> that move events. Not because we consider ourselves a chosen nation; God
> moves and chooses as He wills. We have confidence because freedom is the
> permanent hope of mankind, the hunger in dark places, the longing of the
> soul.[14]

Bush concluded with this peroration:

> History has an ebb and flow of justice, but history also has a visible direction,
> set by liberty and the Author of Liberty. [. . .] When the Declaration of
> Independence was first read in public and the Liberty Bell was sounded in
> celebration, a witness said, "It rang as if it meant something." In our time it
> means something still.
>   America, in this young century, proclaims liberty throughout all the world,
> and to all the inhabitants thereof. Renewed in our strength—tested, but not
> weary—we are ready for the greatest achievements in the history of freedom.
>   May God bless you, and may He watch over the United States of Ameri-
> ca.[15]

President George W. Bush has his share of political critics, and not just
from the Democratic Party. The victorious invasion of Iraq led by the
American president and British Prime Minister Tony Blair ended without

finding dictator Saddam Hussein's store of weapons of mass destruction. Yet Hussein had already deployed WMDs on his own citizens.

Hussein was removed from office and later executed by his own people, but the weapons were never located. If Iraq—after this war liberated them from the Middle Eastern tyrant—ever becomes a viable representative republic, historians will revise their estimate of the younger Bush. In that case, his Second Inaugural Address will rank with Lincoln's as one of America's greatest speeches, echoing Lincoln's phrases from both the Gettysburg Address and the Second Inaugural. The president, along with his neo-conservative writer Gerson, crafted a masterpiece that was heard and read all over the world—including texts smuggled into the totalitarian regimes of Iran, China, and Cuba. It may have inspired revolution in the Middle East, the "Arab Spring"—young people's uprisings against autocratic Arab regimes.

NOTES

1. Remini and Golway, *Fellow Citizens*, 466.
2. Ibid., 467.
3. Ibid., 472.
4. Ibid.
5. Ibid.
6. Ibid.
7. Ibid.
8. Ibid., 473.
9. Ibid.
10. Ibid., 474.
11. Ibid.
12. Ibid., 475.
13. Ibid.
14. Ibid., 476.
15. Ibid

·

Chapter Twenty-Three

Barack Obama, a Promising President?

In U.S. history, there never has been a more heralded presidential inauguration than that of Barack Obama in January of 2009. Americans made their pilgrimage to the nation's capital to witness the historic moment when the first African American would be sworn in as U.S. president.

For American blacks, this was a monumental moment in our history. American slaves had helped build the White House. Now, one who shared their African lineage would reside in the presidential mansion.

It was not just American blacks who perceived in Obama a transformational Messiah. On Super Tuesday 2008, MSNBC's Chris Matthews said, "I've never seen anything like this. This is bigger than Kennedy. [Obama] comes along, and he seems to have the answers. This is the New Testament. This is surprising."[1] *Newsweek* Editor Evan Thomas, appearing on MSNBC's *Hardball* in June 2009, proclaimed, "He's sort of God. He's going to bring different sides together."[2]

Yet Obama's record as president belies that extravagant hope and promise. He said he would bring the Israelis and Palestinians to the negotiating table and create peace. He promised to begin a constructive dialogue with America's enemies in Iran and North Korea and help them see the error of their ways. He pledged to solve the worst economic crisis since the Great Depression.

Obama's one achievement—besides his precedent-breaking election—has been Obamacare. But Obamacare might yet collapse from overpromising and under-delivering. Obamacare that once was the liberals' dream is becoming a nightmare in operation.

The acme of the Obama Administration came in his First Inaugural Address. Never again would hope and belief in this new Messiah soar so high as when he delivered his first speech as president. He read from a speech prepared by Jonathan Favreau. Favreau, a graduate of The College of the Holy Cross, was a former John Kerry speechwriter. A gifted pen, Favreau constructed a paean that ultimately fell short of the day's promise.

Obama opened by thanking his predecessor for his service. Then he opened his address:

> Forty-four Americans have now taken the Presidential oath. The words have been spoken during the rising tides of prosperity and the still waters of peace. Yet, every so often, the oath is taken amidst gathering clouds and raging storms. At these moments, America has carried on not simply because of the skill or vision of those in high office, but because we, the people, have remained faithful to the ideals of our forebears and true to our founding documents. [. . .]
>
> That we are in the midst of crisis is now well understood. Our nation is at war against a far-reaching network of violence and hatred. Our economy is badly weakened, a consequence of greed and irresponsibility. . . . Homes have been lost, jobs shed, businesses shuttered. Our health care is too costly, our schools fail too many—and each day brings further evidence that the ways we use energy strengthen our adversaries and threaten our planet.
>
> These are the indicators of crisis, subject to data and statistics. Less measurable, but no less profound, is a sapping of confidence across our land; a nagging fear that America's decline is inevitable, that the next generation must lower its sights.[3]

But then Obama dismissed President Carter's advice of lowering one's sights:

> . . . the time has come to set aside childish things. The time has come to reaffirm our enduring spirit; to choose our better history; to carry forward that precious gift, that noble idea passed on from generation to generation: the God-given promise that all are equal, all are free, and all deserve a chance to pursue their full measure of happiness.[4]

The audience, full of American blacks, greeted the pledge with great applause.

> In reaffirming the greatness of our nation, we understand that greatness is never a given. It must be earned. Our journey has not been one of short-cuts or settling for less. It has not been the path for the faint-hearted, for those who prefer leisure over work, or seek only the pleasures of riches and fame. Rather, it has been the risk-takers, the doers, the makers of things. . . .
>
> For us, they packed up their few worldly possessions and traveled across oceans in search of a new life. For us, they toiled in sweatshops, and settled the West, endured the lash of the whip, and plowed the hard earth. For us, they fought and died in places like Concord and Gettysburg, Normandy and Khe Sahn.

This is the journey we continue today. We remain the most prosperous, powerful nation on Earth. Our workers are no less productive than when this crisis began. Our minds are no less inventive, our goods and services no less needed than they were last week, or last month, or last year. But our time of standing pat, of protecting narrow interests and putting off unpleasant decisions—that time has surely passed. Starting today, we must pick ourselves up, dust ourselves off, and begin the work of remaking America. [5]

Applause greeted the Obama resolve. Then Obama recited a litany of tasks:

. . . create new jobs . . . build the roads and bridges; the electric grids and digital lines that feed our commerce and bind us together. We'll restore science to its rightful place, and wield technology's wonders to raise health care's quality and lower its cost. [6]

Again, applause greeted Obama's pledges. Applause also met his initiatives, and cut off his final line: "and lower its cost."

We will harness the sun and the winds and the soil to fuel our cars and run our factories. And we will transform our schools and colleges and universities to meet the demands of a new age. [. . .]

The success of our economy has always depended not just on the size of our gross domestic product, but on the reach of our prosperity, on the ability to extend opportunity to every willing heart—not out of charity, but because it is the surest route to our common good. [7]

Again, the audience applauded Obama's high purpose. Obama then turned to foreign policy:

Our Founding Fathers, faced with perils that we can scarcely imagine, drafted a charter to assure the rule of law and the rights of man—a charter expanded by the blood of generations. Those ideals still light the world, and we will not give them up for expedience's sake.

And so, to all the other peoples and governments who are watching today, from the grandest capitals to the smallest village where my father was born, know that America is a friend of each nation, and every man, woman and child who seeks a future of peace and dignity. And we are ready to lead once more. [8]

Again the capital crowd roared their applause.

With old friends and former foes, we will work tirelessly to lessen the nuclear threat, and roll back the specter of a warming planet. [. . .] And for those who seek to advance their aims by inducing terror and slaughtering innocents, we say to you now that our spirit is stronger and cannot be broken—you cannot outlast us, and we will defeat you." [9]

The Capital crowd roared at the Obama resolve.

For we know that our patchwork heritage is a strength, not a weakness. We are a nation of Christians and Muslims, Jews and Hindus, and non-believers. [. . .] To the Muslim world, we seek a new way forward, based on mutual interest and mutual respect. To those leaders around the globe who seek to sow conflict, or blame their society's ills on the West, know that your people will judge you on what you can build, not what you destroy. [10]

Applause greeted the Obama aphorism.

To those who claim power through corruption and deceit and the silencing of dissent, know that you are on the wrong side of history, but that we will extend a hand if you are willing to unclench your fist. [11]

The poetic line triggered applause.

These things are true. [. . .] What is demanded, then, is a return to these truths. [. . .] This is the price and the promise of citizenship. [. . .]

So let us mark this day with remembrance of who we are and how far we have traveled. [. . . .] At the moment when the outcome of our revolution was most in doubt, the father of our nation ordered these words to be read to the people:

"Let it be told to the future world . . . that in the depth of winter, when nothing but hope and virtue could survive . . . that the city and the country, alarmed at one common danger, came forth to meet [it]." [12]

America: In the face of our common dangers, in this winter of our hardship, let us remember these timeless words. With hope and virtue, let us brave once more the icy currents, and endure what storms may come. Let it be said by our children's children that when we were tested we refused to let this journey end, that we did not turn back nor did we falter; and with eyes fixed on the horizon and God's grace upon us, we carried forth that great gift of freedom and delivered it safely to future generations.

Thank you. God bless you. And God bless the United States of America. [13]

NOTES

1. Felix Gillette, "Primary Scream," *New York Observer, observer.com*, published February 6, 2008, accessed September 10, 2015, http://observer.com/2008/02/primary-scream/.

2. Rick Moran, "Blog: Evan Thomas on Obama: 'He's sort of God,'" *americanthinker.com*, published June 6, 2009, accessed September 10, 2015, http://www.americanthinker.com/blog/2009/06/evan_thomas_on_obama_hes_sort.html.

3. Barak Obama, "Address by Barack Obama, 2009/Inauguration of the President" (First Inaugural Address of President Barak Obama, Washington D.C., January 20, 2009), *Joint Congressional Committee, Fifty-Seventh Presidential Inauguration*, accessed July 4, 2015, http://www.inaugural.senate.gov/swearing-in/address/address-by-barack-obama-2009.

4. Ibid.

5. Ibid.

6. Ibid.

7. Ibid.

8. Ibid.

9. Ibid.
10. Ibid.
11. Ibid.
12. Ibid.
13. Ibid.

Bibliography

Adams, John Quincy. *Memoirs of John Quincy Adams.* Philadelphia: J.B. Lippincott, 1852. Quoted in Humes, James C., *My Fellow Americans: Presidential Addresses That Shaped History.* Westport, CT: Praeger Publishers, 1992.

Aitken, Jonathan. *Nixon: A Life.* Washington, D.C.: Regnery Publishing, 1993.

Blum, John Morton. *Woodrow Wilson and the Politics of Morality.* Boston: Little Brown, 1956.

———, ed. *The Letters of Theodore Roosevelt, Volume 6.* Cambridge, MA: Harvard University Press, 1952. Quoted in Humes, James C., *My Fellow Americans: Presidential Addresses That Shaped History.* Westport, CT: Praeger Publishers, 1992.

Boller, Paul F. *Presidential Anecdotes.* New York: Oxford University Press, 1996.

Brands, H.W. *T.R.* New York: Basic Books, 1997.

Brodie, Fawn. *Thomas Jefferson.* New York: W.W. Norton, 2000.

Bush, George H.W. *All the Best. My Life.* New York: Scribner, 1994.

———. "Address Accepting the Presidential Nomination at the Republican National Convention in New Orleans, August 18, 1988." John T. Woolley and Gerhard Peters, eds. *The American Presidency Project, University of California, Santa Barbara.* Accessed July 4, 2015. http://www.presidency.ucsb.edu/ws/?pid=25955.

———. "Debate with Michael Dukakis, September 25, 1988" (Winston-Salem, North Carolina). *The Miller Center, University of Virginia.* Accessed July 4, 2015. http://millercenter.org/president/bush/speeches/speech-5527.

———. "'I Paid for This Microphone': The Reagan v. Bush Debate Controversy" (Debate among Republican Presidential Candidates, Nashua, New Hampshire, February 23, 1980). *NBC Learn K-12 Website, NBCUniversal Media, LLC.* Accessed July 4, 2015. https://archives.nbclearn.com/portal/site/k-12/browse/?cuecard=4511.

Bush, George W. *Decision Points.* New York: Crown Publishers, 2010.

Cannon, Lou. *Jimmy Carter, Man from Plains.* New York: G.P. Putnam, 1982.

Caro, Robert A. *The Years of Lyndon Johnson: The Passage of Power.* New York: Vintage Books (Random House), 2012.

Carter, Jimmy. "Crisis of Confidence — Jimmy Carter" (Text of televised address by President Jimmy Carter, July 15, 1979). *WGBH American Experience, PBS Boston.* Accessed August 26, 2014. http://www.pbs.org/wgbh/americanexperience/features/primary-resources/carter-crisis/.

Chernow, Ron. *Washington: A Life.* New York: Penguin Publishers, 2010.

Churchill, Winston. "The Bright Gleam of Victory" (A Speech at the Lord Mayor's Day Luncheon at the Mansion House, London, November, 10, 1942). *The Churchill Centre.* Accessed September 9, 2015. http://www.winstonchurchill.org/resources/speeches/1941-1945-war-leader/the-end-of-the-beginning.

Clinton, Bill. *My Life.* New York: Vintage Books (Random House), 2005.

Clinton, William Jefferson. "American Rhetoric: William Jefferson Clinton — Oklahoma Bombing Memorial Prayer Service Address, April 23, 1995." *American Rhetoric, Top 100 Speeches.* Accessed August 27, 2014. http://www.americanrhetoric.com/speeches/wjcoklahomabombingspeech.htm.

Davis, Kenneth S. *FDR: The New Deal Years, 1933–1937.* New York: Random House, 1979.

Dean, John. *Warren Harding: The American Presidents Series.* New York: Times Books, Henry Holt and Company, 2004.

Donald, Aida. *Lion in the White House: A Life of Theodore Roosevelt.* New York: Perseus Books, 2007.

Donald, David Herbert. *Lincoln.* New York: Simon & Schuster, 1995.

Flexner, James Thomas. *Washington, The Indispensible Man.* Boston: Little, Brown and Company, 1974.

Ford, Gerald. *A Time to Heal, Memoirs of Gerald Ford.* New York: Harper & Row, 1979.

Ford, W.C., ed. *Papers of James Monroe.* Washington, D.C.: U.S. Library of Congress, Department of Manuscripts, 1904.

Gillette, Felix. "Primary Scream." *New York Observer, observer.com.* Published February 6, 2008. Accessed September 10, 2015. http://observer.com/2008/02/primary-scream/.

Goodwin, Doris Kearns. *Lyndon Johnson and the American Dream.* New York: St. Martin's Griffin, 1991.

Goodwin, Richard N. *Remembering America: A Voice from the Sixties.* New York: Harper and Row, 1988.

Gosnell, H.F. *Truman.* Westport, CT: Greenwood Press, 1980.

Harding, Warren. Address in Woodrow Wilson Park, Birmingham, Alabama, October 26, 1921. Quoted in Dean, John W., *Warren Harding, The American Presidents Series.* New York: Times Books, 2004.

———. Campaign Address in Boston, 1920. Quoted in Dean, John W., *Warren Harding, The American Presidents Series.* New York: Times Books, 2004.

Hechler, Ken. Interview by James C. Humes. Handwritten notes. Marshfield, MO, April 26, 2013.

———. "Truman Library — Ken Hechler Oral History Interview, November 29, 1985" (Interview by Niel M. Johnson). *Harry S Truman Library and Museum Website.* Accessed August 16, 2015. https://www.trumanlibrary.org/oralhist/hechler.htm.

———. *Working with Truman.* New York: Putnam, 1982.

Humes, James C. *Confessions of a White House Ghost: Five Presidents and Other Political Adventures.* Washington, D.C.: Regnery Publishing, 1997.

———. *Eisenhower and Churchill: The Partnership That Saved the World.* Roseville, CA: Forum/Prima Publishing, 2001.

———. Eulogy for President Kennedy delivered to the Pennsylvania Legislature. December 3, 1963.

———. *My Fellow Americans: Presidential Addresses That Shaped History.* Westport, CT: Praeger Publishers, 1992.

———. *The Reagan Persuasion: Charm, Deliver and Inspire a Winning Message.* Naperville, IL: Sourcebooks, Inc., 2010.

Humes, James C., and Jarvis D. Ryals. *"Only Nixon": His Trip to China Revisited and Restudied.* Lanham, Maryland: University Press of America, 2009.

Johnson, Lyndon B. "The Great Society" (Commencement Address to the University of Michigan, Ann Arbor, Michigan, May 22, 1964). *LBJ Library and Museum, The University of Texas.* Accessed August 21, 2014. http://www.lbjlib.utexas.edu/johnson/lbjforkids/gsociety_read.shtm.

Ketcham, Henry. *The Life of Abraham Lincoln.* New York: A.L. Burt, 1901.

Korda, Michael. *Ike, The American Hero.* New York: Harper Perennial, 2008.

Lathem, Edward, ed. *Meet Calvin Coolidge, The Man Behind the Myth.* Brattleboro, VT: Stephen Greene Press, 1960.

Link, Arthur S. *Woodrow Wilson.* Princeton, NJ: Princeton University Press, 1965.

Lippmann, Walter. "The Candidacy of Franklin D. Roosevelt." *The New York Herald Tribune.* January 8, 1932. Quoted in Humes, James C., *The Wit & Wisdom of FDR.* New York: Harper Perennial, 2008.

Lowell, James Russell. *The Complete Writings of James Russell Lowell: Literary and Political Addresses.* Cambridge, MA: The Riverside Press, 1904.

Malone, Dumas. *Jefferson and His Time, Volume 6: The Sage of Monticello.* Charlottesville, VA: University of Virginia Press, 1981.

May, Ernest. *The Making of the Monroe Doctrine.* Cambridge, MA: Harvard University Press, 1975.

McCullough, David. *Truman.* New York: Simon & Schuster, 1992.

Meacham, Jon. *Thomas Jefferson.* New York: Random House, 2012.

———. *American Lion: Andrew Jackson.* New York: Random House, 2009.

Merrill, Horace Samuel. *Bourbon Leader: Grover Cleveland and the Democratic Party.* Boston: Little Brown, 1957.

Moran, Rick. "Blog: Evan Thomas on Obama: 'He's sort of God.'" *americanthinker.com.* Published June 6, 2009. Accessed September 10, 2015. http://www.americanthinker.com/blog/2009/06/evan_thomas_on_obama_hes_sort.html.

Morris, Charles Wilson. *The Monroe Doctrine: An American Frame of Mind.* Princeton, NJ: Auerbach, 1971.

Morris, Edmund. *Theodore Rex.* New York: Random House, 2001.

Nevins, Allen. *Grover Cleveland: A Study in Courage.* New York: Dodd, Mead & Company, 1932.

Nixon, Richard M. "Asia After Viet Nam," *Foreign Affairs,* Vol. 46, No. 1, 111–125, October 1967.

———. "Richard Nixon: Address to the Nation on the War in Vietnam" (November 3, 1969). John T. Woolley and Gerhard Peters, eds. *The American Presidency Project, University of California, Santa Barbara.* Accessed August 22, 2014. http://www.presidency.ucsb.edu/ws/?pid=2303.

Obama, Barack. "Address by Barack Obama, 2009/Inauguration of the President" (First Inaugural Address of President Barack Obama, Washington D.C., January 20, 2009). *Joint Congressional Committee, Fifty-Seventh Presidential Inauguration.* Accessed July 4, 2015. http://www.inaugural.senate.gov/swearing-in/address/address-by-barack-obama-2009.

Padover, Saul, ed. *The Complete Jefferson.* New York: Duell, Sloan, and Pearce, 1943.

Parmet, Herbert S. *The Presidency of John F. Kennedy.* New York: Dial Press, 1983.

Price, Raymond. *With Nixon.* New York: Viking Press, 1977.

Randall, William Sterne. *Thomas Jefferson: A Life.* New York: Harper Perennial, 1993.

Ratnesar, Romesh. *Tear Down This Wall: A City, a President, and the Speech that Ended the Cold War.* New York: Simon and Schuster, 2009.

Reagan, Ronald. "Address Before a Joint Session of Congress on the State of the Union, January 25, 1988." John T. Woolley and Gerhard Peters, eds. *The American Presidency Project, University of California, Santa Barbara.* Accessed July 30, 2015. http://www.presidency.ucsb.edu/ws/?pid=36035.

———. "Address on Behalf of Senator Barry Goldwater: 'Rendezvous with Destiny,' October 27, 1964." *AMDOCS: Documents for the Study of American History.* Accessed August 1, 2015. http://www.vlib.us/amdocs/texts/reagan101964.html.

———. "Remarks at the National Conference of the National Federation of Independent Business" (Washington, D.C., June 22, 1983). *The University of Texas Archives, Ronald Reagan Presidential Library.* Accessed July 31, 2015. http://www.reagan.utexas.edu/archives/speeches/1983/62283b.htm.

———. "Ronald Reagan: Inaugural Address, January 20, 1981." John T. Woolley and Gerhard Peters, eds. *The American Presidency Project, University of California, Santa Barbara.* Accessed August 2, 2015. http://www.presidency.ucsb.edu/ws/?pid=43130.

———. *Speaking My Mind, Selected Speeches.* New York: Simon & Schuster, 1987.

———. "The History Place — Great Speeches Collection: Ronald Reagan Speech on the Space Shuttle Challenger" (Televised address to the nation on the Challenger Disaster, January 28, 1986, alluding to John Gillespie Magee's poem, "High Flight"). *The History*

Place^TM. Accessed August 20, 2014. http://www.historyplace.com/speeches/reagan-challenger.htm.

Remini, Robert V. *The Life of Andrew Jackson.* New York: Harper & Row, 1988.

Remini, Robert V., and Terry Golway, eds. *Fellow Citizens: The Penguin Book of U.S. Presidential Inaugural Addresses.* New York: Penguin Books, 2008.

Roosevelt, Franklin D. "1944 State of the Union Address: FDR's *Second Bill of Rights* or *Economic Bill of Rights* Speech" (January 11, 1944). *Marist College Archives, Franklin D. Roosevelt Presidential Library and Museum.* Accessed August 20, 2014. http://www.fdrlibrary.marist.edu/archives/stateoftheunion.html.

———. "Address at Chautauqua, N.Y. August 14, 1936." John T. Woolley and Gerhard Peters, eds. *The American Presidency Project, University of California, Santa Barbara.* Accessed August 3, 2015. http://www.presidency.ucsb.edu/ws/index.php?pid=15097&st=&st1=.

———. "Campaign Address at Boston, Massachusetts" (October 30, 1940). John T. Woolley and Gerhard Peters, eds. *The American Presidency Project, University of California, Santa Barbara.* Accessed August 3, 2015. http://www.presidency.ucsb.edu/ws/index.php?pid=15887&st=&st1=.

———. "FDR — The Fala Speech" (Campaign dinner address to the International Brotherhood of Teamsters, Chauffeurs, Warehousemen, and Helpers of America, September 23, 1944, Washington, D.C.). *WyzAnt Resources.* Accessed August 20, 2014. http://www.wyzant.com/resources/lessons/history/hpol/fdr/fala.

———. "Fireside Chat" (December 29, 1940). John T. Woolley and Gerhard Peters, eds. *The American Presidency Project, University of California, Santa Barbara.* Accessed August 20, 2014. http://www.presidency.ucsb.edu/ws/?pid=15917.

———. "Franklin D. Roosevelt: Acceptance Speech for the Renomination for the Presidency, Philadelphia, Pa." (Speech before the 1936 Democratic National Convention, June 27, 1936). John T. Woolley and Gerhard Peters, eds. *The American Presidency Project, University of California, Santa Barbara.* Accessed August 5, 2015. http://www.presidency.ucsb.edu/ws/?pid=15314.

———. "Franklin D. Roosevelt: Fireside Chat on Banking" (March 12, 1933). John T. Woolley and Gerhard Peters, eds. *The American Presidency Project, University of California, Santa Barbara.* Accessed August 28, 2015. http://www.presidency.ucsb.edu/ws/?pid=14540.

———. "Franklin D. Roosevelt: Fourth Inaugural Address. U.S. Inaugural Addresses" (January 20, 1945, Washington, D.C.). *Bartleby.com.* Accessed August 20, 2014. http://www.bartleby.com/124/pres52.html.

———. "Franklin D. Roosevelt: Inaugural Address" (January 20, 1937, Washington, D.C.). John T. Woolley and Gerhard Peters, eds. *The American Presidency Project, University of California, Santa Barbara.* Accessed August 2, 2015. http://www.presidency.ucsb.edu/ws/index.php?pid=15349.

———. "Franklin D. Roosevelt, Master Speech File, 1898–1945" (Box 3-14, Draft of Jefferson Day Dinner Speech [last undelivered speech], April 13, 1945). *Marist College Archives, Franklin D. Roosevelt Presidential Library and Museum.* Accessed August 20, 2014. http://www.fdrlibrary.marist.edu/archives/collections/franklin/index.php?p=collections/findingaid&id=460.

———. "Franklin D. Roosevelt Presidential Library and Museum: Our Documents: Lend Lease" (Press Conference of December 17, 1940). *Marist College Archives, Franklin D. Roosevelt Presidential Library and Museum.* Accessed August 20, 2014. http://docs.fdrlibrary.marist.edu/odllpc2.html.

———. "'More Important Than Gold': FDR's First Fireside Chat" (March 12, 1933). *History Matters: The U.S. Survey Course on the Web, George Mason University/City University of New York.* Accessed August 30, 2015. http://historymatters.gmu.edu/d/5199/.

———. "Pearl Harbor Address to the Nation, December 8, 1941, Washington, D.C." *American Rhetoric.* Accessed August 20, 2014. http://www.americanrhetoric.com/speeches/fdrpearlharbor.htm.

———. "President Franklin Delano Roosevelt Fireside Chat, Rattlesnakes of the Ocean, 9-11-1941." *American Merchant Marine at War, usmm.org.* Accessed August 20, 2014. http://www.usmm.org/fdr/rattlesnake.html.

Roosevelt, Theodore. Letter to Oscar King Davis, June 23, 1915. Quoted in Humes, James C., *My Fellow Americans: Presidential Addresses That Shaped History.* Westport, CT: Praeger Publishers, 1992.

Rosenman, Samuel I. *Working with Roosevelt.* New York: Harper and Brothers, 1952.

Salinger, Pierre. *With Kennedy.* New York: Doubleday, 1966.

Sandburg, Carl. *Abraham Lincoln.* New York: Harcourt Brace Jovanovich, 1938.

Shlaes, Amity. *Coolidge.* New York: Harper Perrenial, 2013.

Schlessinger, Arthur. *Age of Jackson.* Boston: Little Brown, 1945.

Smith, Jean Edward. *Eisenhower in War and Peace.* New York: Random House, 2013.

———. *F.D.R.* New York: Random House, 2007.

Sorensen, Theodore C. *Kennedy.* New York: Harper & Row, 1965.

Waldman, Michael. *My Fellow Americans: The Most Important Speeches of America's Presidents from George Washington to Barak Obama.* Naperville, IL: Sourcebooks, Inc., 2010.

White, Philip. *Whistlestop: How 31,000 Miles of Train Travel, 352 Speeches, and a Little Midwest Gumption Saved the Presidency of Harry Truman.* Lebanon, NH: ForeEdge (University Press of New England), 2014.

White, Ronald C. *A. Lincoln.* New York: Random House, 2010.

Wilson, Woodrow. Address to Joint Session of Congress, April 2, 1917. Quoted in Humes, James C., *My Fellow Americans: Presidential Addresses That Shaped History.* Westport, CT: Praeger Publishers, 1992.

———. "U.S. Protest over the Sinking of the Lusitania" (May 13, 1915). *The Lusitania Resource.* Accessed August 28, 2015. http://www.rmslusitania.info/primary-docs/wilson-notes/us-protest-1/.

———. "Woodrow Wilson: Address to Naturalized Citizens at Convention Hall, Philadelphia" (May 10, 1915). John T. Woolley and Gerhard Peters, eds. *The American Presidency Project, University of California, Santa Barbara.* Accessed August 28, 2015. http://www.presidency.ucsb.edu/ws/?pid=65388.

———. Wilson's First Inaugural Address, Washington, D.C., March 4, 1913. Quoted in Humes, James C., *My Fellow Americans: Presidential Addresses That Shaped History.* Westport, CT: Praeger Publishers, 1992.

———. Wilson's Second Inaugural Address, Washington, D.C., March 5, 1917. Quoted in Humes, James C., *My Fellow Americans: Presidential Addresses That Shaped History.* Westport, CT: Praeger Publishers, 1992.

Index

Made in the USA
Columbia, SC
20 December 2017